Also by Mark McCrum

Happy Sad Land
A journey through Southern Africa

No Worries
A journey through Australia

The Craic
A journey through Ireland

Somebody Someday
On tour with Robbie Williams

Castaway
The full inside story of an incredible TV event

GOING DUTCH
IN BEIJING

GOING DUTCH
IN BEIJING

HOW TO BEHAVE PROPERLY WHEN
FAR AWAY FROM HOME

MARK McCRUM

Henry Holt and Company
New York

Henry Holt and Company, LLC
Publishers since 1866
175 Fifth Avenue
New York, New York 10010
www.henryholt.com

Henry Holt® and ® are registered trademarks of Henry Holt and
Company, LLC.

Distributed in Canada by H. B. Fenn and Company Ltd.

Library of Congress Cataloging-in-Publication Data

McCrum, Mark, date.
    Going Dutch in Beijing: how to behave properly when far away from
home/Mark McCrum.
        p. cm.
    Includes index.
    ISBN-13: 978-0-8050-8676-8
    ISBN-10: 0-8050-8676-5
    1. Travel etiquette.   I. Title.
    BJ2137.M33   2007
    395.09—dc22   2007037500

Henry Holt books are available for special promotions and premiums.
For details contact: Director, Special Markets.

First U.S. Edition 2008

Designed by Meryl Sussman Levavi
Illustrations copyright © 2007 by Nick Caruso
Printed in the United States of America

10 9 8 7 6 5 4 3 2 1

Contents

R0024394845

Introduction

The United Nations conducted a global survey. The only question asked was, "Would you please give your honest opinion about solutions to the food shortage in the rest of the world?"

The survey was a failure. In Africa they didn't know what "food" meant; in India they didn't know what "honest" meant; in Europe they didn't know what "shortage" meant; in China they didn't know what "opinion" meant; in the Middle East they didn't know what "solution" meant; in South America they didn't know what "please" meant; and in the United States they didn't know what "the rest of the world" meant.

This little joke, circulated on the Web by disaffected UN staff, points to a central problem of our high-tech, easily spanned globe. Even as we reach a time when a woman in Latvia can communicate in a second with a man in Patagonia and, if she can afford to, fly to see him in twenty-four hours, age-old local manners and attitudes remain deeply rooted. The possibility of making an embarrassing or downright offensive faux pas becomes ever more frequent.

Some intercultural boo-boos will cause little trouble. The fair-minded Finn who insists on "going Dutch" with Chinese business colleagues at a restaurant in Beijing can be tactfully put right; the polite Japanese who arrives at a Parisian dinner party bearing a bottle of fine vintage wine may suffer no worse put-down than a quizzically raised eyebrow; and the Californian who goes out for an evening in Togo wearing beautiful native beads around her neck will be no more than an embarrassed laughingstock. Other mistakes may make for bigger problems. The American businessman who arrives at a meeting in Saudi Arabia wearing a tie covered in amusing pink pigs may well find that he's lost his contract. Likewise, the Englishman who gives the hoot of a fellow driver in Iran a cheery thumbs-up shouldn't be surprised to find himself being run off the road at the next traffic circle.

More innate differences go deeper. However much you tell a Briton or a Swede that forming a line is regarded as a waste of time in Italy, China, or the Middle East, their cultural DNA will still insist that there is something immoral about a person without the basic sense of fairness to wait their turn, while a German who is kept sitting in an outer office for an hour and a half before a meeting in Brazil may find it hard not to treat the lack of punctuality as a personal slight.

The march of globalization is being held up all over the world by similar misunderstandings about the importance of deadlines, the respect paid to rules and contracts, the morality of favoring family over outsiders, and the right work-life balance. There's no escaping these variations in attitude and ways of behaving, which have grown up over centuries and are as attuned to local circumstances as the indigenous flora and fauna.

Ever-increasing travel and migration—not to mention the powerful cross-cultural influences of film and TV—are, of course, changing things everywhere. In Japan people point and catch each other's eye in a way they never used to; new Russians look on the old strictures of *nyekulturny* (uncultured behavior) with an ironic chuckle; in the Middle East young women wear clubbing gear under their *abayas*. But as far as underlying culture is concerned, we do not yet live—as some pundits would have us believe—in a "global village" or a "flat world." Even if most Asians are now thoroughly familiar with the Western handshake and shrewder American businesspeople have learned not to rush things in China, you can still offend a driver on a Greek back road with the wrong kind of held-up palm or cause embarrassment in a Japanese home by stepping on the *genkan* in your socks.

⊕

This book takes a gentle look at everything from first greetings to last rites, covering key areas of potential misunderstanding along the way. Gestures, conversation, clothes, gifts, toasts, eating habits: there are just so many easy ways to offend people—or to be offended yourself. After a look at some of the underlying ways of thinking that can puzzle and confuse the outsider—from the importance of keeping "face" in Asia to the need sometimes for a little *baksheesh* in North Africa—I move on to the cultural differences that can ruin a business trip, before considering what happens if you stay long enough to get involved in a different way: dating, romancing, and even getting married. If you don't do it yourself, perhaps you'll be invited to a wedding—and what, really, could be worse than putting forty thousand yen in the *shugibukuro*? God forbid that you should fall ill or die on your travels, or be the companion of someone who does, but I couldn't resist including some of those attitudes and rituals, too, as well as a glance at the underlying belief systems.

I sincerely hope that by the time you've got to my chapter on good-byes you will no longer look askance at that Japanese gentleman who stares at your shoes when he shakes your hand or sits through your meeting with his eyes closed, nor feel affronted by the African who never says "please" or "thank you." By the same token, that you won't be too extravagant with your gestures in China, that you'll take your coat off in a theater in Russia, and that you'll never hold hands with your partner in Iran (unless they're of the same sex). And if you're invited for a meal at eight o'clock, that you'll turn up on the dot in Cologne, but not till at least nine in Caracas, that you'll leave a little food on your plate in Cairo but never, please, in San Salvador.

Usually, of course, the locals will make generous allowances for outsiders. A friendly manner and a smile will work wonders anywhere in the world. Being genuine and wanting to learn about a culture will get you much further than sticking rigidly to a list of dos and don'ts. But it's surely better to be aware of the pitfalls than not, to know when a ham-fisted attempt to use the local language is going to cause delight (and when offense)—quite apart from how to say *skål* properly or what not to do with chopsticks.

I'm all too aware that many of my observations about other cultures are necessarily generalizations, completely failing to take account of the modest Californian, the loudmouthed Japanese, the feminist Saudi Arabian, the punctual Brazilian, and the snobbish Australian—at least three of which I've had the pleasure to meet. But as anyone who travels knows, sometimes sweeping remarks about a country can be true: for example, if an English person bumps into you, they will generally say "sorry."

One day soon, no doubt, we'll all live in a world that is the global equivalent of the contemporary British high street—grimly uniform and anodyne. Then this book will be a quaint reminder of days gone by. In the meantime, our planet remains a vast and extraordinary place, to the bizarrely varied behavior of which this can be no more than the most modest of introductions.

As they say in South Korea: 즐기십시요!*

* "Enjoy!"

A Note on Spelling

When choosing among the many spellings of foreign phrases, I've usually opted for the most frequently used in the part of the world I'm discussing. However, and particularly when spelling reflects phonetic transliteration from other alphabets, there is rarely only one "right" form. The basic Arabic greeting *Assalamu 'alaykum* ("Peace be with you"), for example, is also spelled *'Salaam alaikum; Salamu 'aleiko* (in Egypt), and *Selâm aleyküm* (in Turkey), to give but three variations; the Russian toast *Na zdorovye* comes out in Poland as *Na zdrowie,* in Bulgaria as *Na zdrave,* in the Czech Republic as *Na zdraví,* in Slovakia as *Na zdravie,* and in Serbia as *U zdravlje.*

If you have any corrections, additions, or local insights, please contact me at http://www.markmccrum.com.

Ha Na?

GREETINGS

Not for nothing did primitive cultures tread warily with outsiders. From the very first moment you set eyes on another human being, the possibility of some kind of misunderstanding arises. To those accustomed to informality, the niceties of our initial dealings with strangers may seem unimportant. But the right way to greet people still varies enormously from one place to another. . . .

Bula!

In Manhattan, London, or Shanghai, saying "Hello" (or *Ni hao*) to a stranger on the street would be seen as odd, even intrusive. If you do so, people are unlikely to reply and will probably assume that you're either a foreigner or a bumpkin from out of town. Outside the self-absorbed bustle of so-called global cities, however, things are more laid-back. Even in the bigger cities of the American south, such as Atlanta, Georgia, people often say "Hi" or "Howdy" to passers-by in the street, as they do in sunny Fiji (where the greeting is *Bula!*). The more local the environment, the ruder it gets *not* to say something. In little towns across France, for example, it's regarded as polite and normal to say *Bonjour, monsieur* or *Bonsoir, madame* to people as you pass by, while those strolling past neighborhood porches in New Orleans would expect to give and receive a "Good evening," even if they're not acquainted.

Ha na?

Africans throughout the continent are generally extremely familiar. In many places it's normal to greet strangers, not just with a "Hi," *Bonjour,* or *Dumela,* but with a follow-up "How are you?" *Ha na?* (West African pidgin), *Habari gain?* (in Kiswahili), and so forth. Mostly this inquiry will be met with a formulaic version of "I am well," and often followed by "And how are you?" which should be answered by a concluding "I, too, am well" before you get on with any other business. In Botswana the sequence goes like this:

Dumela, rra (or *mma,* for a woman)	"Hello, sir (ma'am)"
Dumela, rra. Le kae?	"Hello, sir. How are you?"
Ke teng. Le kae?	"I'm fine. And how are you?"
Ke teng.	"I'm fine, too."

Only now should you say that you'd like a couple of those nice-looking watermelons or ask the way to the center of town.

Farther north, similar ritual questions may well be taken literally, and the polite "How are you?" may be answered by an upbeat or downbeat stream of personal news, to which you're expected to react appropriately. In some places they go even further. As a stranger in rural Cameroon, you won't just be greeted; villagers will stop you and ask you where you're from, how long you've been in the village, who your parents are, if they can help you, and so on. If you're older, and therefore worthy of respect, for strangers not to do this would be seen as actively rude.

Terve!

In stark contrast to all this is Scandinavia. In Sweden it's rarely done to greet an unknown face, even way out in the sticks. In Finland they are similarly taciturn. If they do say hello, there are various levels of salute: *Terve!* or *Päivää!* are formal greetings for strangers; *Hei!* is a friendlier version for those you see more often, and *Moi!* is for those intimates you see regularly.

Discriminating

In India and the Islamic world the greeting of strangers depends very much on gender. In Turkey, if a man joins another man as he is sitting alone on a park bench, he is likely to say *Merhaba* ("Hi") or even the more old-fashioned, formal *Selâm aleyküm* ("Peace be with you"), to which it's polite to reply *Aleyküm selâm* ("And with you, too"). But he would never greet an unknown woman sitting alone.

Women, likewise, will generally speak only to other women, though these days they are unlikely to use the formal *Selâm*, instead saying something like *Merhaba, İyi günler* ("Good day"), or the trendier *Kolay gelsin* ("May things go easily for you") or *Hayirli işler* ("Have a good time at work").

"No harm here"

When Iraq invaded Kuwait in August 1990, the formal greeting Assalamu 'alaykum and its response became a way for residents to reassure themselves that strangers were not dangerous. It took on the meaning "No harm here." Getting a Wa alaykum assalam at a checkpoint meant that you would almost certainly be allowed through without a search.

Equal footing

In the West nowadays people rarely stand up when a newcomer enters the room, but in many parts of the world, from China to Argentina, it would be considered rude not to get to your feet in greeting. Waving from your chair, half-standing, or staring at your shoes just isn't enough.

The bonecruncher

A firm handshake is generally agreed to be a good thing in the West, especially in business circles. But in places as varied as Japan, Costa Rica, and Indonesia, a weak handshake is the norm and is no indication whatever of a lack of assertiveness. This doesn't mean that Westerners have to match limp squeeze for limp squeeze, but it may be wise to tone down the full-on bonecruncher.

Frequency of handshakes also varies. In the United States or United Kingdom one or two establishing handshakes in a group may be enough. In France or Spain newcomers to a meeting will shake hands all around. Nor is this just a business thing. Watch people on a French beach or at a Spanish party, and you'll see the same custom in action—as you will in French-influenced Tahiti and Spanish-speaking Colombia.

4

Invasive

Many Asian cultures are not, traditionally, used to touching as a greeting and have imported the handshake only to fit in with the West. In the Middle East and India, for example, only Westernized Muslims and Hindus will shake hands with the opposite sex. Westerners of either sex shouldn't initiate cross-gender handshaking (a good rule of thumb is never to do so if your new acquaintances are wearing traditional dress).

Orthodox Jews, likewise, may be put out if a person of the opposite sex extends a hand. For a man, the problem is that the woman may be *niddah* (menstruating), not something he can tactfully inquire about; for a woman, if her head is covered, indicating she's married, she shouldn't shake hands (or embrace) at all.

Acceptance

Africans often go in for elaborate handshakes as a sign of friendship or solidarity. In west and central Africa men will shake hands, then, as they pull their palms away, grasp the other's middle finger between their thumb and forefinger and snap it. Farther south the "African handshake" is a three-part affair: the handshake begins normally and is followed by an upward clench before ending back as before (they'll show you how). To be offered this as a visiting white person—*muzungu*—is a big sign of acceptance (particularly in South Africa).

Northern Africans will often tap the left-hand sides of their chests with their right hands after a handshake, to show that they take your greeting to their hearts. In Chad sincerity is indicated by the left hand reaching out and supporting the right elbow from below as you shake, a charming action that's also found in South Korea.

In Senegal, merely extending a wrist or elbow is perfectly polite if you're already holding something, while women in

Guatemala and Nicaragua are more likely to pat each other on the forearm than shake hands.

Frau first

In Germany always make sure you shake hands with the wife before you do so with the husband. In a large group—say at a restaurant—newcomers may rap their knuckles on the table in greeting rather than reach out and actually shake all the paws around the table.

Rebonjour

When the French see each other for a second or third time in the same day, they greet each other with the delightful expression *Rebonjour.* But when they've shaken hands once, that's it for the day.

Eye to eye

In the West children are often taught to look adults in the eye when shaking hands. Direct eye contact is considered a sound accompaniment to a handshake, indicating sincerity. In Mediterranean, Arab, and Latin American countries the gaze may be so full-on it disconcerts. But don't be offended if, in other parts of the world, your new acquaintance doesn't return the favor. In both Japan and Vietnam eye contact is generally avoided, as it is in China, where too long a look is considered disrespectful.

In the Australian outback full-blooded Aboriginals will tend not to meet your eye at all until a firm and trusting relationship is established. In central and southern Africa eyes are often averted when speaking with elders or superiors; in west African Ghana children are taught *not* to look adults in the eye at first meeting: to do so would indicate defiance.

Smiley

In the United States and the United Kingdom it's polite to smile when you first meet someone; however false or creepy the grimace, the attempt signifies that you're at least trying to be happy about the encounter. But grins of greeting are not universal. Especially when it comes to business, many cultures regard meeting someone new as a serious matter. So take your cue from your new acquaintance: if they smile, smile back; if not, keep it straight.

If Japanese or Indonesians grin or laugh, it may not mean that they find what you're saying funny—it's just as likely that they don't understand something or are embarrassed.

Salaam

Full-on Arabic greetings can be highly elaborate. After the initial *Assalamu 'alaykum* exchange—accompanied by a gentle handshake—you may then pull back your hand and touch your heart. A traditional host may now place his left hand on your right shoulder and kiss you on both cheeks. Don't initiate this, but if it happens, you should reciprocate. If your host subsequently holds your hand, for however long, don't pull yours away. This is not a come-on (perish the thought, in a part of the world where homosexuality is still a capital offense) but a straightforward gesture of friendship. Subsequently, making any form of religious gesture is flattering. Saying *Inshallah* ("God willing") is respectful and will always go over well.

Be careful about what you admire, be it a watch, tie pin, or beautiful ornament: a more traditional host may feel obliged to give it to you and take offense if you refuse, after which—and here's the rub—you're expected to present him with a gift of equal value. So, if you feel the urge to compliment your new friend on his diamond-encrusted Rolex, do so obliquely.

Pecking order

Though Swedish or Australian egalitarians may scoff, in many cultures the *order* in which you greet people is still highly significant. In Venezuela, for example, you should always introduce yourself to the oldest person first, while in status-conscious Indonesia it's the most important you should honor. In China, the highest-ranking visitor will walk into the room ahead of his party and lead the greetings, and the Japanese are equally big on the right pecking order.

Such niceties have been largely swept away in the West, though in very grand and formal situations—meeting royalty, for example—the less important should still, technically, be introduced to the more. So: "Your Majesty, may I introduce Mr. Smith," *not* "Mr. Smith, this is the Queen."

Ojigi and *namaste*

The traditional Japanese greeting is, of course, the *ojigi* (bow). If a Japanese meets a fellow countryman, he will bend from the waist, eyes lowered, to the same level—or lower, if the person he's addressing is more important. Men keep their arms to their sides; women rest their hands on their thighs, fingers touching.

The days when *gaijin* (Western visitors) were expected to bow in return are long gone. In Japan today you will be greeted with a Western handshake. Stick with that. If you try and do anything else, you risk getting it wrong. If you should find yourself bowed to without a handshake (when exchanging cards, perhaps, or in a rural area), a polite nod back will suffice.

Indians also have a tradition of bowing, known as *namaste,* where in addition the palms of the hands are held together near the heart as one says *Namaste* (pronounced nam-a-stay).

Foreigners may reciprocate in kind, but if it makes you feel silly, this is not a requirement. For Western women greeting men in India, however, a respectful *namaste* can be a useful way around the dilemma of whether or not to shake hands.

Thais have a similar gesture, which they call the *wai*—the higher you hold your hands, the more respect you're showing. The precise etiquette is complex, so for an outsider the *wai* is best avoided.

Les bises

Yes, men do kiss each other abroad—but never on first meeting. Even serious kissers such as the Russians are quite formal with strangers. The bear hugs and damp smooches come later, when you are established colleagues or friends.

The English are often a bit awkward with social kissing— men more so than women, although they go along with it because it's sophisticated and Continental. The sophisticated and Continental French, of course, have no such hang-ups: they routinely do *les bises*, a double air-kiss to the cheek, and would regard it as rather cool or detached *not* to kiss. Belgians and single Brazilian women kiss three times; in Latin America the third kiss is supposedly for good luck in finding a spouse.

In Egypt they kiss each other on the forehead, and in Benin friends of the same sex may greet each other with several kisses, ending with a light touch on the lips. In Italy it's not regarded as creepy for a man to bend to kiss a woman's hand, while in conservative circles in Germany and Austria a charming older man may mutter as he raises a lady's hand to his lips, *Küß die Hand* ("I kiss your hand"). In Vietnam or China, by contrast, even a peck on the cheek or forehead is verboten; in rural areas women who've been observed kissing a man have been driven to suicide by the shame.

The breath of life

The Maori of New Zealand ritually greet each other with the *hongi*, pressing their noses and foreheads together to share the same breath, which is known as the *hā* (breath of life). As a stranger, once you've shared breath, you cease to be thought of as one of the *manuhiri* (visitors), but become one of the *tangata whenua* (people of the land). A similar greeting still applies across the scattered islands of Polynesia, where the nose kiss is known as the *honi;* when entering a hut to offer this, remember always to keep your head lower than your host's, especially if he is the chief. Put your nose on his knee or shin, then wait for him to bring your face up to his. On the far side of the Pacific, in Hawaii, this nose kiss is still the *honi,* and the—often offensive—word for outsider, *haole,* means, literally, "without the breath of life."

Earth mother

In Maori folklore, the first woman was created by the god Tāne, child of Ranginui (the Sky) and Papatūānuku (the Earth), who molded her out of red earth. He then embraced her and breathed into her nostrils, at which point she sneezed and came to life. Her name was Hineahuone (woman formed from the earth) and she and Tāne later had a daughter called Hinetītama, the Dawn Maiden, who was to control the change from darkness to light.

A present from the gods

Visitors to the South Pacific may be charmed by the custom of a welcoming *lei*, or garland of scented flowers, being placed around their neck as they arrive on their island of choice. In these days of mass travel this is more likely to happen to people on upmarket tours than to every backpacker who passes through.

In Hindu culture, likewise, it's traditional after greeting someone to hang a garland around their neck. If this happens to you in India, there's no need to go on wearing your adornment indefinitely; once seated, remove it and put it to your right on the table. If offered a garland by a stranger at a temple as a *prasad* (present from the gods), be aware that the stranger will expect you—not the gods—to pay for it.

Sit on This!

GESTURES

The power of the gesture is extraordinary: hold your two fingers around one way as you wait for someone to drive past you on a narrow road in the United Kingdom, and they'll smile broadly, happy that you're not only polite but also peace loving; hold them the other way around, and they'll be out of their car running purple-faced across the tarmac to strangle you. Yes, when you leave the familiar certainties of home behind, it's all the more crucial to be careful. The wrong gesture offers the very fastest shortcut to cross purposes and hostility. . . .

The cheery thumbs-up sign, so encouraging and upbeat in the United Kingdom or Sweden, will get you sworn at or worse if used in a traffic jam in Iran, where it means, literally, "Sit on this!" There the gesture is known as the *bilakh* and is an unquestioned insult, equivalent to using the raised middle finger at home. In India, it can also be rude, if accompanied by the word *"thengaa"* (coconut) or *"angutachap"* (illiterate). Children in particular are fond of these insults.

OK

The American sign for "OK," in which the forefinger touches the top of the thumb to make a circle (with the other fingers loosely bent), has many different meanings around the world. In the south of France, Portugal, Italy, Greece, and Zimbabwe it means "Zero" or "No good," while in Japan it's a sign for money. The blandness stops there. In Iran it's the sign of the evil eye, while in places as different as Turkey, Malta, and Brazil the gesture suggests that you are comparing someone to the filthiest part of their anatomy. Do the "OK" to a traffic cop in Istanbul and expect a big fine at the very least. Interestingly, this same action has been adopted internationally in scuba diving to mean, when unable to speak in potentially dangerous circumstances several fathoms deep, "I'm fine." How this works in the waters off Ilha Grande is anybody's guess.

Two fingers

Americans should also be careful about using the "victory" sign in the United Kingdom, where two fingers held up in a palm-inward V will lead them to discover the limits of the famous

British sense of humor very quickly indeed. The gesture has the same meaning as "F—— off" in Australia and Ireland. And with the simple addition of a nose poked between the parted fingers it's equally rude in Mexico and Saudi Arabia.

Palm outward, however, the gesture is inoffensive everywhere. It can mean a laid-back, hippyish "Peace," a more gungho, Churchillian "Victory," or simply "Two," as in "Two more beers, please."

Intact

The V sign is said to date back to the Hundred Years War between France and England. Captured archers, the story goes, would have the two main fingers of their right hand cut off to prevent them from ever drawing a bow again. So the gesture arose as a soldier's way of indicating that he was still intact and ready for action. A twist on this possibly apocryphal story has the triumphant English archers of Agincourt (October 1415) marching past French prisoners and flicking them the Vs in triumph (which may explain why the sign means both victory and "F—— off"). Interestingly, the Churchill Archives Centre in Cambridge has photographs of the wartime leader using the iconic gesture of defiance both ways. And Margaret Thatcher, trying to copy her hero, famously got it backward at the Woolwich by-election of 1975.

Hook 'em horns

Another gesture that has very different meanings around the world is the "hook'em horns" (index and little finger up, thumb pressed onto curled-back middle fingers), used by President George W. Bush during his second inaugural ceremony in 2005. Down home in Texas, this is the victory sign of the University of Texas Longhorns. In most of the rest of the world exactly the same gesture has less salubrious meanings. In Norway it's the sign of the devil, while in Italy it's known as the *cornuto* and suggests that a man is a cuckold—a profound insult, even if untrue. Whether the culturally sensitive world leader was aware of these other readings when he went on international TV with the "hook'em horns" is not known.

I love you

The horns should not be confused with the "I love you" gesture, beloved of American rock stars, televangelists, and politicians. This has the index and little finger raised and the two middle fingers folded over. The difference is that the thumb and little finger (or "pinkie") are spread out in a big, loose V.

The finger

There is no place on the globe where raising a single middle finger (and perhaps jabbing it aggressively at your counterpart) is polite. It's supposed to symbolize the erect penis and means, universally, "F—— off." The gesture dates back to Roman times, when it was known as the *digitus impudicus* (the rude finger).

Arabs generally do it upside down, with the fingers splayed and the middle finger raised a little and pointing straight down.

The arm of honor

Slapping one hand on the other upper arm while raising the lower arm in a fist is as phallic as "the finger" and offensive pretty much everywhere. In France it's nicknamed the *bras d'honneur* (the arm of honor).

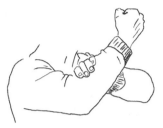

The fig

A variation of the above skips the arm slapping and has the thumb poking out from between the index and middle finger of a closed fist. Known in some places as the *figa* (fig), it is effective in giving offense in Korea, Russia, and many Mediterranean countries— Turkey and Greece in particular. In Brazil and

Venezuela, however, the very same gesture means "Good luck," and you can even buy a beautiful *figa* pendant, featuring a replica of the gesture in solid silver, to hang around your neck. Just remember to take it off before your next trip to Seoul or Moscow.

Crossed fingers

There are plenty more chances for misunderstanding with this one. In Europe and some parts of the USA, crossed fingers means either "good luck," "let's hope so," or "looking out for you" (while fingers held crossed behind your back indicate that you don't mean what you're saying). But in Russia, showing crossed fingers is a way of rudely rejecting or denying something, and in Paraguay and Uruguay it's as offensive as the *figa*. In Spain

and Argentina the sign is made to ward off bad luck, while in
China it signifies the number 10.

The *moutza*

Holding out your palm toward someone, so unobjectionable in most parts of the world, where it could be a wave, a sign to "stop" or even a thank-you, may well get you into trouble in Greece, where the gesture—known as the *moutza*—is deeply insulting. The offensiveness dates back to the days when chained criminals would be paraded around town and have cinders (*moutzos*) and excrement wiped in their faces as a form of public humiliation. The closer you put your hand to someone's face, the more threatening it's considered. Two palms are more offensive than one, and if you add one or two feet you are really pulling out the stops.

Le Camembert

The French have a range of gestures all of their own, from the Indifferent Gallic Shrug to the Indifferent Gallic *Moue* ("pout") and back again. *Le Camembert* is a useful one: hold your hand in front of you in an L, then slowly bring thumb and forefingers together, as if grasping a piece of soft cheese; accompanied by a studied expression of vast indifference, this is a rude way of telling a Frenchman to shut the f—— up.

Les Boules is another good one: hold a pair of imaginary balls in front of your chest and twist your face into an expression of—yes, always indifferent—frustration. This means, in the most satisfyingly superior way possible, "I've had enough."

Palm flicking

Flicking your hand, palm downward, toward the ground, means "Never mind" in the United States and most of the rest of the world; but in Latin America this dismissive little flutter suggests that someone is gay. In the 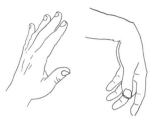 birthplace of heterosexual *machismo*, this is an easy way to start a fight.

Best foot forward

Bear in mind that in addition to deliberate gestures, even casual, familiar movements can cause problems. Folding your arms in front of your chest in Finland is regarded as rude and standoffish, as it is in parts of the United States. Putting your hands on your hips is seen as a sign of aggression in countries as far apart and different as Kenya, Nicaragua, and Malaysia. Across the Middle East it's fine to cross your legs, but if by doing so you point the sole of your foot at someone, that is, traditionally, an insult; in Arab cultures the feet, always in touch with the filthy ground, are considered unclean.

This taboo about feet extends east to Buddhist countries,

Arch heel

When Iraq fell in 2004, the locals vented their anger at Saddam Hussein by beating his effigy with the soles of their shoes, which was about the rudest thing they could do. Just a year and a half later, in December 2005, Prime Minister Ayad Allawi, widely seen as an American stooge, was chased from the shrine of Imam Ali in Najaf by a hail of shoes and sandals.

---

where the foot is also considered the most impure part of the body. Stepping on a bank note in Thailand, for example, would be regarded as particularly disrespectful, as you'd be treading on the image of the much-revered king.

The evil eye

In Buddhist countries you should never pat someone on the head, in however friendly a fashion. The head is considered to be sacred—the seat of the soul—and touching the top of it is highly insulting, even for a child.

In Mexico the reverse is true. A common belief is that if someone sees a beautiful child they *have* to touch them, usually on the head or the face, or else something bad will happen to them. As they touch they say *No le vaya a hacer ojo* ("I don't want to provoke a curse on him/her"). Mexican mothers are often stopped in this way as they push their baby carriages around the streets.

Beware, however, of joining in with this practice as a visitor from another country. If a total stranger, particularly with blue, green, hazel, or other light-colored eyes, touches or looks at a child in the wrong way, they are believed to be sending *el mal de ojo* (the evil eye).

To the point

Children in the United States and United Kingdom are taught that it's rude to point, but the index finger is quite often used by adults to indicate things. Be careful about doing this, though, in the Middle and Far East and in many parts of Africa, where pointing at anything with a single finger is frowned upon. Use a fully open hand instead.

Malaysians point with a closed fist, the thumb at the top indicating direction. Filipinos are even more low-key, singling out an object by shifting their eyes toward it or pursing their lips and pointing with their mouth. Venezuelans, likewise, may use their lips to point. In west African Guinea-Bissau they take this a step further, gesturing with their chin or tongue; this is one place in the world where it is more polite to stick out your tongue than raise your finger.

Come hither

Be wary, too, of beckoning with a single, crooked finger. In both Yugoslavia and Malaysia this is a gesture reserved for animals, while in Indonesia and Japan it's just plain rude. Throughout Continental Europe, the Middle East, and much of Latin America the gesture for "Come over here" is to extend the arm, hand out, palm down, and make a scratching motion with the fingers. In Japan, this is more of a waggling motion; in fact, it can look very similar to the English one for "Go away."

Neh and okhee

Those from places where yes and no are indicated by a nod or a shake of the head may easily assume that such essential gestures hold true the world over. They'd be wrong.

Albanians and Bulgarians nod their head to say no and shake it to say yes. In Sri Lanka, similarly, the wobbling movement of the head from left to right and back again is an encouraging or affirmative gesture (which can be catching after a while), while the straight nod of the head up and down is a negative one.

In Turkey people toss their heads backward and raise their eyebrows to say no. A similar upward movement of the head also means no in Greece and Arab countries (where it is sometimes accompanied by a click of the tongue). In Greece, just the raising of the eyebrows can be enough to indicate a negative, and the words don't help much either: *neh* is the Greek for "yes" and *okhee* means "no."

In Spain or Latin America, if a man winks and whistles at a woman, it's not an insult. This sort of cheeky street approval is called the *piropo* and may well be accompanied with a verbal compliment, along the lines of *Hola guapa!* ("Hello, gorgeous!"), *Qué piernas!* ("What legs!"), or *Diosa!* ("Goddess"). If the lady ignores it, it will be taken no further, though a gracious smile accepting the compliment will always go over well, without implying any desire for a follow-up.

In Australia a man winking matily at another man is fine, but to wink at a woman, even to indicate that a joke has been made, is not done and may get you into trouble out in the sticks, where the more unreconstructed Aussie male really doesn't like you getting too close to his sheila. In Saudi Arabia, winking at anyone is considered vulgar, and in Hong Kong it's downright rude.

Eating the scraps

Though something of a dying art these days, longer and more sophisticated piropos *display all the imagination of the incorrigibly flirtatious male:* Si la belleza fuera delito, yo te hubiera dado cadena perpetua *("If beauty were a crime, you would deserve life in prison");* Con lo que se te ve y lo que se te imagina, yo ya tengo bastante *("With what you show, and I imagine, I have enough")* Si tu cocinas como caminas, quiero comer las sobras *("If you cook like you walk, I want to eat the scraps"). The very well-practiced may even indulge in the indirect* piropo, *spoken to the mother of a beautiful young woman as they pass by in a pair:* Me gustaría que Usted fuera mi suegra *("I wish you were my mother-in-law").*

Space invaders

North Europeans and Americans like their personal space. In Latin America, North Africa, the Middle East, and China, by contrast, people often stand so close that you can feel their breath on your face. If you edge away, they'll probably try to close the gap. The polite thing is to adjust and accept their alarming proximity. Otherwise, if you move away, they'll follow, and so on, till a slow and embarrassing chase around the room ensues.

Many people in these "space-invading" cultures will gravitate toward other people as a matter of course. If you're sitting alone in a movie theater or on a bus in Egypt, for example, a new arrival may well cross the intervening gap to take the seat next to you. Don't misinterpret this herding instinct; it doesn't necessarily mean that he wants to talk to you.

Mongolian footsie

In Mongolia, if you step on someone's foot, you're expected to shake their hand and offer to let them step on your foot in return. It can be an odd experience in a crowded bus in Ulan Bator to find an old woman begging you to press your boot on her shoe.

Mr. Man

NAMES

Time was when a person's name revealed all sorts of important information about them: where they were from, whether they were single or married, what generation they belonged to, even who their parents were. Now, in a world of mass population movement and intercultural union, nothing can safely be assumed. Samantha Chaudhuri may turn out to be a dyed-in-the-wool suburban London girl who married a British Indian, or an adventurous Bengali who's adopted the European given name she first took on at a call center in Mumbai. By the same token, Wesley Chan may sound like a funky Afro-Asian but turn out to be an inscrutable Dubliner with a thick Irish accent. . . .

Great to meet you, Mr. John

In the Far East the correct order of names can be confusing. Calling Mr. Li Wong Chee of Singapore "Mr. Chee" is like calling Mr. John William Smith of London "Mr. John." In general, the order is reversed, with the surname first (Li), then a name that indicates belonging to a particular generation (Wong), then a given name (Chee). If you are lucky enough to be invited home to meet Mr. Li's wife, bear in mind that Chinese women do not take their husband's surname, so if her name is Ho Chu Chin, she will be known as Madam Ho.

Things are never simple. In Taiwan, thanks to the influence of missionary schools, many people have a Christian forename preceding their local names, which then follow in the usual Eastern order. So Mr. Johnnie Li Wong should be called Mr. Li (Johnnie Li to his chums). The situation has been further complicated by increasing contact with the West. So as not to confuse foreigners, many Easterners now change the order of their names. So Mr. Li Wong Chee may, after all, really be Mr. Chee Wong Li, and should be correctly addressed as Mr. Chee.

Confused? If in doubt, it's always fine to ask.

Lions and princesses

Hindus in the north of India generally have a given name (or two) followed by a family surname, which often indicates caste, usually by describing a traditional occupation (Gandhi, for example, means "grocer" or "pharmacist" and Patel "tenant farmer"). Recently, there have been protests against these caste-related names and some people no longer use them.

In the south, people didn't traditionally have surnames at all. A Hindu man used the first initial from his father's name, followed by his own given name. Both were often preceded by an initial indicating his hometown. So K. V. Sanjeev would be Sanjeev, son of Vidvan, from Kokradi. With many this practice

Mrs. Kim

In his 1993 state visit to South Korea, President Bill Clinton addressed his hosts, President Kim Young Sam and his wife, repeatedly as President and Mrs. Kim. However, Korean wives don't follow Japanese tradition and change their name when they get married; they keep their maiden names. So President Kim's wife, Sohn Myong Suk, should correctly have been addressed as Mrs. Sohn. As Clinton had arrived straight from Japan, his failure to get this right suggested—in a land where "keeping face" is everything—that Korea was not as important as Japan. A serious no-no.

still continues, though the first initial is often dropped, and some more modern individuals lose the initials altogether and use their given name followed by their father's name. Women do the same but, after marriage, will drop their father's initial or name and add their husband's after their given name. So when J. Ranjana (Ranjana, daughter of Jaidev) marries K. V. Sanjeev, she becomes Mrs. Ranjana Sanjeev.

Sikhs have a given name followed by *Singh* (for a man; it means "lion") or *Kaur* (for a woman; it means "princess"), after which may sometimes come a clan name. You should call a Sikh by their title and first name: *Sardar,* abbreviated as *S,* is the equivalent of "Mr."; so Jasbir Singh would be known as Mr. Jasbir or S. Jasbir. To call him Mr. Singh would be absurd, like calling someone "Mr. Man" in the United Kingdom or United States.

From the house of . . .

Though some Indian and Pakistani Muslims retain Hindu clan names, such as Patel or Chaudhuri, in general Muslim names derive from Arabic. In the Arab world a Muslim is known by his

MR. MAN

given name plus *bin,* which literally means "from" but usually stands for "son of." After that may come a grandfather's name and, in some countries, a family name. So Dr. Osman bin Sultan bin Ahmad al-Harithi is Osman son of Sultan, grandson of Ahmad, from the house of Harithi. (You should call him Dr. Osman.) When it comes to his lovely sister Zeinab, her female ancestors are of no consequence. She is Zeinab bint Sultan bint Ahmad al-Harithi (or *binti* in some places; both mean "daughter of"). When she marries, she doesn't change her name; only informally is a wife called "Mrs.," followed by her husband's first or last name.

In most Gulf Arab countries the *bin* or *bint* is replaced by the alternative *ibn* or dropped altogether, so you are left with a bare string of male ancestors, which may continue beyond the grandfather: Osman Sultan Ahmad Abdallah al-Harithi. Throughout the Muslim world the preliminary title *Hajji* is an honorific for those who've made the *hajj,* or pilgrimage to Mecca.

Umm

As people in the Middle East are routinely addressed by their first name, you may not know how to match your Arab counterpart when the time comes to move from surnames to given names. If people have children, a nice way around this is to start addressing them by using the name of their oldest child and *Abu* (father of), or *Umm* (mother of). So Osman now becomes Abu Abdullah, and his wife, notionally, Umm Abdullah—though in practice such intimacy is unlikely.

War and peace

As far as names go in Russia, not much has changed since Tolstoy. The Russians have their given name first—say, Vasily or Yekaterina—then the patronymic, which is their father's name—Alexei, for example—modified by an ending meaning "son of"—Alexeyevich—or "daughter of"—Alexeyevna. Then comes the surname—Borodkin, say, giving us Vasily Alexeyevich Borodkin. In addition, a woman adds a female ending to her name, so she becomes Yekaterina Alexeyevna Borodkina. Leaving this gender indicator out is not a good idea; it's the equivalent of calling a woman "Mr."

Among themselves, Russians shorten these name mouthfuls with numerous diminutives and nicknames. Don't join in until they ask you to; you will then probably be expected to use the first name and patronymic, which indicates both friendliness and respect. At this point you may invite them to use your first name, too.

If you want to skip the first name and patronymic you may use the titles *Gaspodín* (Mr.) or *gaspazháh* (Mrs.), which are pretty much reserved for use by foreigners. The term *tovarisch* (comrade), popular in Soviet days, is now totally out of fashion and would only ever be used ironically—at, say, a committee meeting: "Shall we hear what Tovarisch Borodkin has to say?"

One hundred years of total confusion

Those who've read the novels of Gabriel García Márquez or who have spent time in Latin American countries know that the norm is to have two given names—say, Ana María or José Antonio. In writing or in formal situations, the father's surname follows, then the mother's, giving us Ana María or José Antonio Vásquez Rodríguez. For normal day-to-day purposes Ana and José should be addressed by their title, followed by their father's name: Señor or Señorita Vásquez. If and when Ana marries, she may add her husband's name to the list—generally preceded by "de"—and drop her maternal surname, so she now becomes Ana María Vásquez de Martínez, addressed as Señora de Martínez or, less formally, as Señora Martínez. If she doesn't marry, she remains Señorita till she drops; to call her Señora would be to cast doubts on her virginity. José, however, does not add his wife's name to his list when he gets hitched.

MR. MAN

Thoughtful South Americans sometimes make things simpler for outsiders by underlining on their business cards the names they should use. And remember, just to add to the fun, in Portuguese-speaking Brazil the father's name, rather than the mother's, comes last.

San

Never address a Japanese by his first name, which is used only by his family and very close friends. Use his (or her) last name and add the word *San* (Mr./Mrs.).

Herr Doktor Professor

Whatever the name, attached titles should always be treated with care. In informal cultures—such as the United States, Israel, Sweden, and Australia—referring to someone as "Doctor" or "Professor" may not matter much, indeed could even be regarded as pretentious or stuck-up. But this casual attitude doesn't translate to places that on the surface may seem equally (or more) laid-back. You might expect titles to be important in Germany, France, or Japan—and they are—but professional people in Italy, Spain, and Latin America are just as keen to be called *Dottore* (Doctor), *Abogado* (Advocate, that is, Lawyer), or *Ingeniero* (Engineer) as the Germans are *Herr Doktor* and *Frau Professor*. So stick to Señor, Sheikh, Princess, and so on until you are asked not to.

You and you

Be careful with languages that have formal and familiar forms for "you." In some places the distinctions no longer matter. In the Netherlands, for example, they regard it as friendly to use the familiar *jij* or *jullie;* the formal form—*u*—is reserved for business correspondence and children. Few French people will care if a foreigner *tutoyers* them in ignorance, although they would expect you to get it right if you claim to be fluent (among themselves the familiar form is reserved for family, friends, pets, and insults). And in Spain only older people would expect *usted* rather than *tú*.

But in Germany, the formal *Sie* and familiar *du* forms should not be confused. Not so long ago the newspapers ran a story about a woman who was arrested for saying *du* to a policeman. This was hardly typical but points to the truth that it can take a long time to get on a first-name basis with a German; if you try and rush the process, you may seem overly familiar, if not rude.

Drink to brotherhood

Traditionally, changing from formal to informal modes of speech in Germany was marked with a special ceremony— the Brüderschafttrinken (Drink to Brotherhood). Two men would toast each other with a stein of beer, link arms, and formally invite each other to be as familiar as a brother, a custom that continues to this day in some places.

Butch and Poochy

Like Americans, Thais use first names right off the bat. Even at first meeting you may be called Mr. Mark or Miss Susan. Filipinos, by contrast, love using nicknames—Peachie, Butch, Bing-Bong, or Poochy—which sound pretty strange to outsiders. But when a Filipino invites you to call him by his nickname, you should do so, and then ask him to call you by yours, even if this involves making one up. Filipinos in the police or military also enjoy mock-flattering one another by upgrading their ranks. So a police constable may be jokingly called

"Captain," or an army captain "Major." As an outsider, you are not expected to join in with this tomfoolery.

Old Uncle

Nicknames are also popular in Africa. In Niger people call one another by nicknames in preference to real names, which are never used. They refer to one another instead by relationship or occupation (for example, Old Uncle, Vegetable Seller, and so forth). It's taboo also for a woman to use the name of her husband, or for anyone ever to use the name of a dead relative or friend.

Indigenous cultures sometimes have the oddest taboos in this area. Among the Sanema people, who live deep in the Amazon jungles of Venezuela, for example, it's forbidden to address anyone by their given name. The way around this is to use their alternative Spanish name.

Joking cousins

In Mali people who share the same last name (which generally refers to a family occupation—farmer, storyteller, and so on) are called *sanangouya,* or "joking cousins," even if they've never met before. By long custom this special relationship means they're free to tease and abuse one another when they meet, saying perhaps that A smells, B is ugly, or whatever. Sometimes *sanangouya* don't even have to share a surname to join the fun: a Kouyate, for example, may joke in this way with a Keita.

The upside of all this is that *sanangouya* can also get tangible benefits from their "relatives." A police officer is likely to be more lenient with a joking cousin, for example, or someone may invite a homeless joking cousin to live in their house.

Lao and *xiou*

When you get to know your Chinese counterpart a little better, a nice, informal way of addressing each other is by using his surname along with *Lao* (old) or *Xiou* (young) in front of it. People start being addressed as *Lao* in their midthirties, so don't take it personally if you're Lao Jones rather than that perfectly toned young buck, Xiou Jones. Console yourself: in China they respect their elders and betters.

Conversation Stoppers

WHAT NOT TO SAY

In general it's best when traveling to avoid politics, except in a spirit of tentative, open-minded inquiry. Telling people they live in an interesting or beautiful place will always go over well. Sports are another safe subject, though beware of the new foreign acquaintance who knows more about your national games than you do; he may think you're a bit of a wimp when you fail to keep up. In all cultures you can rarely go wrong with family and food: "What beautiful children you have" or "This rat cake is delicious" are surefire ways to anyone's heart. . . .

Too close for comfort

Be careful, in particular, about discussing adjacent countries. Nothing enrages a certain kind of Irishman more than to be described as British, or a nationalistic Scot more than being called English. Whatever they say, New Zealanders don't like being mistaken for Australians, and Canadians hate to be thought American (especially if they're wearing one of those little maple-leaf badges). Indians won't be happy if you confuse them with Pakistanis, Bangladeshis, or Sri Lankans, while Bolivians don't warm to praise of any of their neighbors—having lost wars with all of them.

"What's the best way to make a fortune?" ask the Uruguayans. "Buy an Argentinian for what he's worth, then sell him for what he thinks he's worth."

Made in the Republic of China

In China keep off current events and indeed anything controversial. Political no-nos include, of course, Tibet, as well as referring to Taiwan as the Republic of China, or, worse, "Free China." In Arab countries be wary of talking about the Persian Gulf: many prefer to call it the Arabian Gulf (*al-Khalīj al-Arabī*).

PBUH

Talk about sex is a taboo in Muslim countries, and dirty jokes a total no-no. If mention is made of the Prophet Muhammad, either in speech or writing, it should be followed by the words "Peace be upon him," which is generally shortened to "PBUH" in written communications.

Smörgasbored

Being critical of the country you're visiting, even in jest, is a mistake: Scandinavians, for example, get very weary of outsiders telling them how high their cost of living is. They know.

More conversational pitfalls

Australia	talking disparagingly about Aboriginal people
China	human rights; Tibet, Taiwan; sex; religion; bureaucracy
Far East	confusing Japanese, Chinese, or Koreans, in any combination
Greece, Cyprus	asking for Turkish coffee
India	poverty; sex; dowry deaths (see page 140)
Ireland	referring to Great Britain as "the Mainland"; talking about "the British Isles" to include Ireland; asking why they use euros rather than pounds sterling
Latin America	using "Americans" to refer to just North Americans
Mexico	nepotism
The Netherlands	calling the country "Holland" (inaccurate and offensive to people not from the Holland provinces)
New Zealand	using the term "the Mainland" for either North or South islands; mispronouncing Maori place-names
Northern Ireland	asking people whether they're Catholic or Protestant
Russia	corruption, contract killings, and so forth.

South Africa	going on and on about apartheid (it ended some time ago)
Spain	criticism of bullfighting
U.S. South	the Confederate flag

When in Rome

. . . do as the Romans do remains wise advice. But don't take it too far. Copying local ways of behaving can render you ridiculous. Many Argentinians summon waiters with a loud, lips-macking kissing noise, but this wouldn't go down well if it came from an outsider. Australians say "G'day" to each other but can react oddly when they hear the greeting repeated by visitors, especially if they detect any hint of mockery; Americans from the Deep South feel the same way about outsiders copying their drawling use of "Y'all."

In Singapore the locals speak "Singlish," an English-based creole that incorporates elements from Chinese, Baba Malay, and Indian English. Although it's fine to make an effort to understand this rich, slangy, street language, with its emphatic *lah* and *mah* at the end of sentences and its South African–style "Isn't it?" added to direct questions, you would be regarded as preposterous if you came out with *Dis guy Singlish si beh powderful wan—hoh seh liao, lah!* (literally, "This person's Singlish is very good").

Bangalored

A similar slang that should be treated with caution is "Hing-lish," the mix of Hindi and English that is common in the cities of India (and has now spread to those of the United Kingdom). Once distinguished by quaint, Raj-relic usages, such as "poppy-cock," "the needful," and "felicitated," it now embraces hip modern coinages: British call-center workers whose jobs have been outsourced to India have been "Bangalored," while sexual harassment is referred to as "Eve-teasing." In the process, some colonial-style words have reemerged as thoroughly pukka.

achha	Is that so?
airdash	in a hurry
angrez	English person
badmash	crook or hooligan
buck	rupee, pound
chaa	tea
chuddies	underpants (as in "Kiss my chuddies," catchphrase of UK TV show *The Kumars at No. 42*)
filmi	behaving like a character in a Bollywood movie (as in "very filmi")
glassy	in need of a drink
jungli	uncultured
kati	I'm not your friend anymore
prepone	opposite of postpone; to move something (such as a meeting) forward
rasmalai	a sweet; thus, an attractive woman
tik	fit, attractive

Other cross-cultural slang phrases are springing up all over the place and are best avoided. To the hip youth of Thailand, to "chill-chill" is to "relax," and "hiso" (from "high society") means "posh." And let's not forget the hybrid language of Hong Kong: Honklish.

Bonjewer Monsewer

The temptation for thoughtful visitors to try and speak the host language can be strong, and the gesture is often appreciated. In countries such as Denmark or Botswana, where the native language is unlikely to be used elsewhere, the clumsiest *Tak* or

Dumela will bring a smile for your effort. Russians, too, love it if you try to speak their language.

In other, prouder cultures inadequate efforts may only annoy. Those who've tried to speak bad French to a busy Parisian waiter will understand this. In France in general, unless you speak good French with confidence, your counterparts would probably prefer you to speak English clearly—after a short apology for not being able to speak French, of course. By the same token, in international airports it may be clear from the weary expression of your coffee server that they'd rather you just said "Thank you" in English than hesitate for ten seconds with your cash while you try and remember if it's *Gracias* or *Obrigado*.

The risk of getting it badly wrong is always there, particularly with languages such as Chinese or Japanese, where correct pronunciation and tone are crucial. Your carefully rehearsed

---

La Francophonie

The French are famously protective of the integrity of their language, which ruled supreme as the lingua franca of international diplomacy and educated people from the sixteenth to the early twentieth century. In 1635 Cardinal Richelieu founded the Académie Française, with the aim of laying down clear rules for the language and keeping it pure. Regional patois (dialects) were banned, and children could be beaten in school for using them. In 1994, in the latest of these restrictions, le Loi Toubon ("the Law of Toubon," named after the then culture minister) required that all product descriptions, advertisements, instructions, and public signs in France must be in French. In 1996 the English cosmetic firm Body Shop was duly fined for using the English terms "no frizz" on a hair treatment and "pineapple" about a facial cleanser.

CONVERSATION STOPPERS

phrase or toast may come out meaning something entirely different, like that of the Americans who thanked their Chinese hosts with the prepared line, "Thank you very much for the dinner. I am so full I must loosen my belt," which poor pronunciation rendered as, "Thank you very much for my dinner. The girth of your donkey's saddle is loose."

I wait with patience

In France, questions of the "Are you married?" or "Do you have children?" variety would be considered far too personal on a first meeting. But in the Arab world these are the appropriate things to ask about. In Asia, likewise, you may quiz people about their age, the age of their spouse, even how much that watch on their wrist cost—subjects that would be out of order in supposedly forthright North America. In the Far East such inquiries can be even more intrusive. "How much money do you earn?" or "How large is your house?" would not be considered beyond the pale in Vietnam, Japan, or the Philippines.

In Africa you may have to accept not just questions of the "Are you married?" variety but advice, too. "Why are you not married?" may be followed by a long insistent wail of "You *must* marry. You must have *children*. Who will inherit your *house*, your *car*?" and so on. In Muslim countries at least there is a useful answer for this kind of approach: "Allah has not blessed me yet. I wait with patience."

Sabra

Israelis are famously direct. They may not only ask you extremely personal questions but also weigh in immediately with advice. "How much did that suit cost you?" could easily be followed by, "You paid too much." Don't let this or any other form of brusque public behavior bother you: Jews born in Israel refer to themselves as *sabra,* which is the name of the indigenous

Blin

For those of us who are used to men and women who curse at
the smartest occasions, and who perhaps make a point of swearing in order to show that they are real, streetwise, down with
the kids, or whatever, it may be hard to fathom that in many
cultures swearing is unacceptable—certainly so in mixed company. Even in tough-talking Russia a woman would never use
an expletive; she is more likely when upset to say *blin* (a kind of
sweet pancake), the equivalent of saying "sugar."

The magic words

Many African languages have no words for "please" and "thank
you," but this doesn't reflect an ingrained rudeness; it's more
that such statements are seen as unnecessary between individuals who already have a powerful obligation to provide for each
other. A similar bluntness can be found in Germany and Scandinavia, where pussyfooting around with extra little attempts to
ingratiate is seen as unnecessary. In all these places it's all too
easy to fall into thinking that everyone's rude—when from
their point of view they're just being clear and to the point.

Whingeing Poms

Certain cultures use teasing as a way of establishing friendship.
Argentinians may be surprisingly derogatory about your weight
or choice of clothes, but don't take offense: it just means they
are relaxing with you. Australians, similarly, may have a go at
pretty much anything. Don't take it personally: tease back,
within careful limits. It's OK for an Aussie to call an Englishman
a "whingeing Pom" and be rude about his country's warm beer,

terrible weather, or lamentable cricket team, but criticize *his* wine, his culture, or pretty much any aspect of the native sporting ability of his fellow countrymen and the laughter may suddenly stop.

Be careful, likewise, of joining in with self-deprecating cultures. A liberal Israeli in Tel Aviv may laugh at the "beardy-weirdies" of Jerusalem, or an Egyptian mock the tiresomeness of his bureaucracy, but you crack your own jokes about these things at your peril.

Divided by a common language

Never forget that even within a single language, words have different meanings in different places. In Spain *Adios* means "Good-bye"; in Cuba the same word is used on the street as a "Hi, hello" to passersby. In France *Bonjour* means "Hello"; in Quebec, people say it as they leave. In Spain a *tortilla* is a thick omelette with potato; in Mexico it's the flat bread in which you wrap food. In Portugal, *bicha* is a "line"; in Brazil it means "gay." If you are *constipada* in Lisbon, you have a cold; in Rio you have a long time to read the newspaper in private. Talk about "great crack" in Dublin and they'll know you're having a good time; in Detroit they may think you're trying to sell them rock cocaine.

Fanny pack

The worst Old/New World mix-ups probably occur in that "special relationship" between the United Kingdom and the United States. Brits traveling to the States should be careful never to say to someone at a party, "Excuse me, could I bum a fag off you?" while Americans traveling to the old country should remember that "pants" are not the leg-covering garments that the British call "trousers"; they are the altogether more intimate and skimpier underclothes (and the word itself has become slang for "rubbish"). Nor does "fanny" refer to what the English call, variously, a bottom, backside, or bum: it's slang for an altogether more intimate part of the female body. Telling an English person they're wearing "great pants" or asking for a "fanny pack" in an English drugstore may draw strange looks—if not outright giggles.

Other possible misunderstandings across the pond

English	American
aubergine	eggplant
bum	fanny (noun)/borrow (verb)
(car) bonnet	hood
(car) boot	trunk
(car) exhaust	muffler
cravat	ascot
digestive biscuit	graham cracker
dinner jacket	tux(edo)
ex-serviceman	veteran
fag	cigarette/gay man (rude slang)
full stop	period
grill	broil
lift	elevator
public school	private school
pram	baby carriage
roundabout	traffic circle
secretary	clerk
solicitor	attorney
sweets	candy
toilet/lavatory	restroom/bathroom
tramp	bum
trainers	sneakers
Underground, Tube	subway
vest	undershirt
waistcoat	vest

Thank you for your toilet paper

The Japanese imported their system of writing from the Chinese, which has led, in later years, to occasional confusion: the Japanese character (or kanji*) for "thank you" resembles the Chinese one for "disastrous"; Japanese "daughter" looks very like Chinese "mother"; and the* kanji *for "letter" resembles the Chinese character for "toilet paper."*

A good root

Many of the great intercultural faux pas have to do with the unintended use of slang words for sex. Telling an Australian you're "rooting" for them or their team at an Aussie Rules match may not be the wisest thing to do: the word is slang for having sex ("a good root" is not a turnip). Stand beside a beautiful young couple in Brazil and say *Caliente, no?* and you'll be innocently talking about the weather; in Spain the guy will think you fancy his girlfriend. Nor will asking a German *Bist Du heiss?* ("Are you hot?") be taken as a question about their body temperature.

White Socks and Chrysanthemums

CLOTHES AND GIFTS

Clothes send out strong signals to people you're meeting for the first time, so be careful that those signals are not read differently abroad. In the United Kingdom a man wearing white socks outside a sporting context might be seen as tacky or flashy, but in Switzerland even the smartest businessmen wear them with business suits. In Stockholm a man in a pink sweater is elegantly dressed; in a bar in Alabama he might be thought effeminate. And the American executive who walks into a meeting in Saudi Arabia wearing a novelty tie embellished with flying pigs is almost certain to cause offense—the pig is unclean in the Muslim world.

Boho

In many cultures what you wear is an indication of your status. Businesspeople who slope around the office in crumpled suits or tatty sneakers should bear in mind that in places such as Belgium, Turkey, or Brazil, where dress matters, they will be judged by their appearance. In Arab and many African countries, by the same token, the concept of "boho chic" is incomprehensible: people simply wouldn't understand why a well-off person would dress down or deliberately badly. If you can afford decent clothes, why wouldn't you wear them?

Bella, bella

In Italy the concept of *la bella figura* (the beautiful figure) comes close to being a national trait. Italians aim to look their best at all times, dressing up and putting on makeup even if they're just popping out to the shops. On summer evenings, in the *centro storico* (historic center) of towns across Italy, the gentle public stroll known as the *passeggiata* is a chance for people to show off everything from their new shoes to their new girlfriend. As a tourist, you won't be expected to join in, but if you're staying for longer than a vacation, at least trying to cut your own version of *la bella figura* will get you taken more seriously. Italians always notice shoes: keep 'em shiny.

Provocative statement

For women, sartorial freedom is a long way from being a world standard. It goes without saying that short skirts and low-cut tops are out of order in Muslim countries. In Saudi Arabia such garb might well attract a whack on the shins from the stick of a passing mullah, possibly backed up by accompanying *mutaween* (religious police). Sleeveless tops are borderline, and pants should be worn under a long blouse that covers the hips.

But don't go the whole hog and adopt Arabic dress. If a Western woman turns up in head scarf or *abaya* (the traditional black robe), the assumption would be that she's either married to a Gulf national or is intending to be.

The *mutaween*

Saudi Arabia's feared "religious police," the mutaween *(also known as the Commission for the Promotion of Virtue and Prevention of Vice), are empowered to enforce total compliance with the country's fundamentalist sharia laws. They roam the streets of the kingdom checking on dress codes and sex segregation and making sure that prayers are performed on time. In March 2002 the* mutaween *received unprecedented public criticism when they stopped schoolgirls leaving a burning building in Mecca because they were not correctly dressed in headdress and abaya. Fifteen girls died and more than fifty were injured in the blaze.*

Going native

Wearing what the locals wear can be OK up to a point. Donning the semitransparent decorated shirt known as the *barong Tagalog* in the Philippines is fine for any social occasion, as is the open-necked, long-sleeved *batik* shirt in Indonesia. The Burmese claim to appreciate Westerners who try on the traditional, skirtlike *longhi* (even as they themselves switch to imported, Chinese-made denims), and it's quite acceptable for visiting women to wear the loose, pajamalike *salwar kameez* in Pakistan.

But the risk of causing offense or appearing ridiculous is always there. South Americans will not be impressed by Europeans who turn up to the evening *asado* (barbecue) dressed as a *gaucho* (pampas cowboy) or in native Indian costume. Wearing local beads as jewelry in Togo could also make you a laughing-stock: they are traditionally worn at the waist to hold up an underskirt. To hang them around your neck is much the same as putting your underwear on your head.

Slip-ons

Old-fashioned rules of English etiquette dictated that you should never wear brown shoes with a dark suit. But in most parts of the world, whether you wear black lace-ups, white slip-ons, or fake crocodile-skin loafers, the fact that you keep your footwear on causes more offense than its appearance. In most Arab homes a guest should remove shoes before stepping inside—you can tell if this is necessary as there will be a pile of boots and sandals or a rack at the door. Always take off your shoes in mosques and Buddhist temples, and don't just leave them any old way; place them neatly together, facing the door you came in at. When visiting a Japanese home, leave your footwear in the *genkan* (area outside the front door), toes pointing toward the exit, before stepping into the house. You will be given slippers to take you from the front door to the living room, where they should be removed before you step on the *tatami* (reed mat). On a visit to the restroom you'll be given separate "toilet slippers."

It's always a good idea in such countries to wear nice, clean socks. Before you leave, check that you've got the right shoes: confusion is all too easy, and it's a bore to realize when you get back to the hotel that you're wearing Mr. Yamazaki's brogues.

Chinese sandals

Socks worn with sandals may be thought tacky these days at home, but in China they're de rigueur. Bare feet, even if encased in the hippest designer wear, are not acceptable.

Czechiket

According to Ladislav Špaček, one-time spokesman for Czech president Václav Havel, and coauthor of a 2005 Czech etiquette manual, forty years of communism left the Czechs with a distinct lack of style and social grace. "It was a big setback. Under communism, people would just wear sweatpants and overalls." Among Špaček's hot sartorial tips for his fellow countrymen are "Hats should always be worn slightly tilted to one side." "If someone's dress is unzipped, let them know in a tactful manner." "Fur coats don't look good on everyone—especially men."

Present imperfect

The giving or not of presents when abroad is another area fraught with problems. In some places, such as Japan, it borders on the compulsory. In others, such as the Netherlands, bringing a gift for a host or business associate would be regarded as unnecessary, even a bit of a waste of your time and money. In between these extremes lie many different shades of obligation and many pitfalls. . . .

Paper knives and antique clocks

You may be unlikely to give someone a pair of scissors or a knife, but if either of these does occur as a brilliant idea, be aware that in places as different as China and South America such a gift would symbolize the cutting-off of your friendship or business relationship. In Brazil, Argentina, and Peru, handkerchiefs connote grief, while for the Chinese you can add straw sandals and clocks—all three are items associated with funerals. Superstitious rural Cantonese may even take the present of a clock to mean that you're counting the seconds to the recipient's death.

WHITE SOCKS AND CHRYSANTHEMUMS

Made in Bordeaux

Consider where you are before you choose your gift. South America is awash with cheap leather goods, so a finely tooled wallet may not seem quite so special. Koreans will not be impressed with a gift marked "Made in Korea." Taking a bottle of wine to a French dinner party is not merely carrying coals to Newcastle: your host may feel obliged to serve your bottle. If it's of poor quality or, *Mon Dieu!*, New World, he (and the other guests) may be embarrassed for you. If it's the best money can buy, it may put to shame his careful selection of vintages from the truly remarkable *petit vignoble* that only he has as yet discovered.

Colorful insults

Pay heed, too, to the religion and superstitions of your destination country before you choose your *cadeau*. Alcohol is clearly a no-no in Muslim countries; likewise cowhide leather goods in India, where the cow is sacred. Other cultures attach great significance to color. Red, gold, and silver are all auspicious colors in China, but white and black are associated with funerals, blue is the color of mourning, green is unlucky, and a present wrapped in yellow paper with black writing is given only to the dead. The best way to avoid problems is to buy in your destination country and get your choice wrapped in a local shop.

What can you buy for $19.99?

Be particularly careful if there's any business or political context to your generosity. In places such as Malaysia or Paraguay, where corruption is an acknowledged problem, gifts that could be construed as bribes are frowned upon. In China and Singapore government employees are not allowed to accept any gifts ever, while the U.S. government limits the value of presents received by its federal employees to $20.

Flowers may seem like the perfect thing to take along to delight the gracious hostess of the dinner you've been invited to, but beware: in many countries particular varieties, colors, and even numbers have unwelcome associations. Lilies are used at funerals in countries ranging from Costa Rica to the Philippines, while chrysanthemums are a reminder of death in Belgium, Italy, France, Spain, and Turkey. Other flowers to be avoided include:

red roses	Austria, France, Germany; Philippines	suggest a romantic interest; too personal
dahlias	Spain	associated with death
frangipani	Singapore, Malaysia, India	associated with death
marigolds and carnations	Thailand, Sweden, Poland, Germany	used for funerals
red carnations	Austria	reserved for May Day
anything purple; yellow	Bolivia	used for funerals; signifies contempt
anything yellow	Mexico, Chile, Eastern Europe; Russia, Iran	a sign of grieving or separation; signals displeasure, hatred
anything white	Japan	associated with death
anything yellow; red; white	Mexico	connotes death; casts spells; lifts spells
even number	Germany, Japan, Austria, India, Turkey; Russia	bad luck; for funerals only

WHITE SOCKS AND CHRYSANTHEMUMS

odd number	China, Taiwan, Indonesia	bad luck
wrapped in paper	Sweden, Germany, Poland	considered rude
anything except roses	Peru	regarded as cheap
any	Kenya, Tanzania	for condolences only

It's nothing

In Japan presents are a key part of life, enshrined in the very language: instead of saying, "You helped me," the construction is "I receive the gift of you helping me." The Japanese give each other gifts at New Year's, during a special season in the summer, on birthdays, and on numerous other occasions. If you're staying with Japanese people or working with them, at some point they'll expect to exchange a little something with you. Don't give too early on in your visit, but if your host hands you a gift, you should aim to reciprocate as soon as possible.

Your present should be in a box and/or beautifully wrapped, ideally in paper of a pastel color. Recent corruption scandals mean that super-expensive presents for business contacts are to be avoided; choose something simple and stylish. Give with both hands and suggest that what you're offering is unimportant compared with the relationship you are honoring. Your Japanese counterpart will do likewise, possibly using the phrase *Tsumaranai mon* ("It's nothing") or suggesting in other ways that the gold-plated MP3 player they've just handed over is really nothing special. Individuals should be presented with gifts in private; if giving to a group, gather them together and have something for everyone. Handing out a present to only one member of a group would be thought rude.

A little something

There are thirty-seven separate occasions during (and after) a Japanese life when ceremonial gifts are given. These include birth, the first new year of a baby, first birthday, entering school, being promoted a grade, graduating, reaching adulthood, finding a job, getting married, becoming pregnant, retiring, celebrating longevity (at ages 61, 70, 77, 80, 88, 90, and 99), funerals, hoji (memorial services), and anniversaries after death.

You really shouldn't have

Giving—and receiving—gifts with either the right or both hands is important throughout the Middle East and Asia; in China, as in Hong Kong or Japan, it should always be with both hands.

In China, Hong Kong, or Singapore someone may "graciously refuse" a gift three times before accepting it; ideally, you should do the same. In all these countries—and Japan—you should never encourage your recipient to "Go on! Have a look!" The potential disappointment of receiving something they don't need or want could lead to an unbearable loss of face. In most other places, from Sweden to Chile, you would expect a gift to be opened in front of you, and fulsome thanks to follow, even if the recipient privately hates your thoughtful present of a coffeetable book full of delightful pictures of your hometown.

Kiondo

In Kenya, if you bring a present with you to a meal as a thankyou, you will gain cultural brownie points if you place it in a *kiondo,* a traditional woven bag made from sisal, often decorated with glass beads. At the end of the evening your *kiondo* will be given back to you with a little present in it—and possibly, too, some leftover treat from the meal you've just eaten.

What not to buy

	Good gift	Bad to disastrous gift
Arab countries	a beautiful compass (useful for finding Mecca)	a pigskin wallet; an erotic print; fine cognac; a dog
Argentina	fine whisky (single-malt Scotch); perfume for a woman	a knife in a leather case with a corporate logo
Brazil	a meal out; a bottle of good French wine; orchids	a bottle of *cacacha* (the local cane spirit)
China	a banquet; fine cognac; a nice pen (but not one containing red ink)	a clock
Colombia	fine liqueur or brandy	anything with a corporate logo (regarded as cheap)
France	flowers; chocolates	a bottle of wine, especially New World; anything with a logo
India	a nice box of pastries	a belt made from cowhide; a leather jacket
Japan	fine European cognac or Scotch whisky; a nice pen	a beautiful engraved knife (suggests separation)
Korea	American ginseng	anything that says "Made in Korea"

Mexico	flowers; chocolates; European wine	Californian wine; anything silver (considered too common)
Russia	a favorite CD; a case of fine wine	a bottle of vodka
Venezuela	orchids (the national flower); gold jewelry	handkerchiefs (represent sadness)

Branded

Even though gifts with corporate logos are often seen as less than impressive, branded goods, particularly from grand and well-known shops, may go down surprisingly well. An item in a Saks Fifth Avenue box or in the famous turquoise Tiffany packaging may be just what you need to impress, from the Caribbean to Kyoto.

Flagging the offense

To mark the state visit to China in February 1989 of George H. W. Bush, Premier Li Peng gave the U.S. president a bicycle— a thoughtful gift as Bush loved bicycles and had spoken warmly of his days cycling while in China as the U.S. ambassador. In return Bush gave Li Peng a pair of Texan cowboy boots, with one sole showing the Chinese flag and the other the Stars and Stripes. But in Asia, of course, the sole of the foot is considered the lowliest and most unclean part of the body.

WHITE SOCKS AND CHRYSANTHEMUMS

Oogy Wawa!

TOASTS AND DRINKS

The cementing of acquaintance, friendship, or the success of a business deal with a shared drink is something that happens in almost all cultures, even where alcohol is not drunk. (In Islamic countries tea or coffee will be offered.) If only it were as simple as picking up your glass and putting it to your lips. . . .

Getting your toast right is a potential minefield. *Cin cin* (pronounced "chin chin") may sound fine in Galicia, Tuscany, or even a pub in London but may not be quite the thing in Tokyo, where *cin-cin* is a word that a mother might use to her little boy in the bath to describe a certain key part of his anatomy.

Skull!

The words of most toasts center on wishing "good health" or "long life" to your surrounding acquaintances or friends. The Scandinavian *skål,* however, is more sinister, originating from the Viking custom of drinking from the empty skull of a recently conquered enemy. To do this toast properly, you should raise your glass in an arc from waist to lips, while looking your host directly in the eye. Then say *Skål,* drink, and make a wave of the glass before your host's face, before bringing it back down to the table, always keeping that eye contact. If you're gathered in a group, even if your shot is poured and waiting temptingly on the table in front of you, everyone must wait for the host to say *skål* before drinking.

Bad sex

There are local variations on toasts everywhere. In Switzerland you must clink glasses with everyone within reach before drinking. In Japan you should never fill your own glass; wait for your neighbor to offer, and when his is half-empty fill it in return. In China, if your host proposes a toast, you must immediately reciprocate with one of your own. In Germany an old superstition holds that if you don't look into your counterpart's eyes when clinking glasses, seven years of bad sex will follow.

OOGY WAWA!

The right glasses

The basic German equivalents of "Cheers!" or "Your health!" are *Prost!* (for beer) or *Zum Wohl!* (for wine). But personalized toasts may be longer or more formal: *Ich möchte einen Toast auf Hermann ausbringen!* ("I'd like to propose a toast to Hermann!") More elaborate toasts are used on special occasions and may even include humor:

Hoffentlich hast du soviel Spaß an deinem Geburtstag, daß du ihn von nun an jährlich feierst! "I hope you have so much fun on your birthday that you celebrate it annually from now on!"

Hundert Jahren sollst du leben und dich freuen, und dann noch ein extra Jahr—zum Bereuen! "May you live a hundred years, with an extra year to repent!"

Das Leben ist bezaubernd, man muß es nur durch die richtige Brille sehen! "Life is wonderful, you just need to see it through the right glasses!"

Interestingly, many of these German toasts have their origins in Ireland, where the capacity for inventing whimsical drinking salutations is second to none: "May you live as long as you want, and never want as long as you live"; "May the Lord keep you in his hand and never close his fist too tight"; "If you're lucky enough to be Irish, you're lucky enough!"

Tamada

In Georgia and Azerbaijan toasts can often go on throughout an entire meal. This is no random affair, especially at a *supra* or feast. A specific person is designated—or sometimes just assumes—the role of *tamada* (literally, "father of all") or toastmaster. It's up to the *tamada* to know who everyone is and to introduce each one of them with a suitably exaggerated encomium, praising their business success, empathy with other people, cooking skills, or whatever else it is that sets them apart. Sometimes the toast may take the form of a little story with a surprising punch line that refers back to the person being toasted. Individual toasts can last ten to fifteen minutes, and, as everyone at the table has to be included, the full formal session can go on for hours. As a visitor, you will be honored first; then, traditionally, come the elderly *aqsaqqals* (white-bearded men) and *aghbircheks* (white-sideburned women) and so on down in order of importance. Having received your paean of praise, be sure to sit quietly through the rest of the ceremony. Talking to your neighbor, or even drinking, while toasts are being made is not regarded as good manners.

Shine and the *Titanic*

Among both Jamaicans and urban African-Americans, "toasting" means something rather different. Jamaican "toasts" are the "verbals" MCs add over music, ranging from squeals and screams to full-on commentaries or improvised storytelling, often rhymed in a rap style. African-American toasters, meanwhile, retell black legends. One famous old toast, "Shine and the Titanic," relates the heroic attempts of Shine, a black stoker on the doomed ship, to warn his captain of the approaching disaster. More contemporary toasts may focus on cynosures of the local urban community.

Buttocks up!

Though many toasts are a version of "Good health"—such as the French *Santé* and the Irish *Sláinte*—some have other meanings. The Japanese cry of *Banzai* ("Long life"), is matched by the Jewish *Le Chaim* ("To life"). The English "Bottoms up" finds echoes around the world. In Greece *Aspro pato* means "White bottom" (of the glass); in Slovakia they say *Až do dna*, which loosely translates as "All the way to the bottom"; and in Hawaii *Okole maluna* means a literal "Buttocks up."

Toasts are often very similar throughout a particular region—even if the countries of that region have been historically at one another's throats. *Skål,* for example, is the right thing to say throughout Denmark, Sweden, Norway, and Iceland (though in Iceland you may also say *Samtaka nu*).

In Russian you say *Na zdorovye* (with the stress on the first *o* and the rest mumbled), while in Poland it's *Na zdrowie,* in Bulgaria *Na zdrave,* in the Czech Republic *Na zdraví,* in Slovakia *Na zdravie,* and in Serbia *U zdravlje.* Versions of *Salud* or *Salut* work well across southern Europe and into linguistically related South America. In Italy it's *Salute;* in Spain, Mexico, and Spanish-speaking Latin America it's *Salud;* Portugal and Brazil have the softer *(A Sua) Saúde.* In the Netherlands you can go two ways: *(Op uw) gezondheid,* which is the same in Belgium and among the Dutch-originated Afrikaners of South Africa; or *Proost,* which becomes *Prost* in Germany and Austria.

Other toasts

Language	Toast
Armenian	*Genatzt* (pronounced Genatsoot)
Basque	*Topa*
Bengali	*Joy*
Chinese	*Kong chien / Wen lie / Ganbei*
Finnish	*Kippis*
Georgian	*Gaumarjos*
Greek	*Yamos / Iss Ighian* (old-fashioned) */ Gia Sou*
Greenlandic	*Kasugta*
Hawaiian	*Hipahipa / Hauoli maoli / Okole maluna*
Hindi	*Apki lambi umar ke liye / Mubarik*
Hungarian	*Kedves egeszsegere*
Indonesian	*Selamat minum*
Korean	*Konbe / Kong gang ul wi-ha yo*
Maori (New Zealand)	*Kia-ora*
Thai	*Chai-yo*

To the ladies

In Russia the second toast is generally *Za zhenshchin* ("To the women"). Though it's undoubtedly cheesy, a bit like an Englishman saying "To the ladies," learning this or another toast in Russian will always go over well.

The silent toast

It is a tradition in the U.S. Navy that a toast never be made with water, as this is said to condemn the subject to a watery grave. In the United Kingdom the annual "Immortal Memory" toast is drunk by the Royal Navy on Trafalgar Day (October 21) to honor the memory of Admiral Lord Nelson, the victor of that famous day in 1805 when the British defeated the allied navies of the French and Spanish at sea. After saying the words "The Immortal Memory of Nelson and those who fell with him" (or simply "the Immortal Memory"), the toast is drunk in total silence.

I'm not as think

In Finland, Poland, and Russia spirits are the drink of choice. Your hosts will ply you with vodka and expect you to get drunk, though they will of course admire you if you turn out to have a harder head than theirs. Remember, in Russia, once a vodka bottle has been opened, it must be finished—and a toast means the draining of a full glass. "Do you *rezz-bekt* me?" your inebriated host will inquire, even as he asks you to join him in another. If

OOGY WAWA!

you want to at least try to stay sober, make sure you eat plenty of *zakuski* (snacks) between shots.

In the United Kingdom, Ireland, Australia, and parts of the United States, similar attitudes to heavy drinking prevail. Many an early evening pub or bar conversation will revolve around the drunken antics of the last session, and legendary boozers—Peter O'Toole, George Jones, Bette Davis—are spoken of with admiration.

. . . as you drunk I am

Farther south in Europe they are more modest with their use of alcohol. A French dinner party may well center around a fine *bouteille* or two, but when they are finished the party will happily move on to *tisanes* (herbal teas). And spoiling the palate with a pre-prandial martini is regarded as very bad form: an *apéritif* should at least be in the *style* of the wine that is to follow. As in France, in Italy drunkenness is regarded as the height of bad manners, though recently a younger generation has been following Northern European trends, and broken glass and pools of vomit can be seen on streets where once there was nothing more than a sedate and sociable *passeggiata*.

Suiyi!

The Chinese will expect you to drink a lot. If you don't want to follow *Ganbei!* with the customary single gulp, say *Suiyi!* ("As you like!"), which allows each of you to sip instead.

Backhanded

Latin Americans have a series of bizarre taboos about wine pouring, so it's probably best to wait for your glass to be filled. Pouring with the left hand, for example, is considered rude, as is tipping a bottle backhandedly.

Shouting

When out with a group in Australia—as in the United Kingdom—it's important always to "shout your round" (that is, buy drinks for everyone present). Visiting teetotalers and light drinkers need not worry: this tradition is about sharing, not compulsory drunkenness, and as long as you get everyone what they want, it's perfectly OK to drink orange juice all night.

Seasoned round buyers will know that a wise strategy is to buy early, before the cost of the ever-expanding group's drinks becomes prohibitive; the only danger of this ruse is if you're still at the table when it's your turn again. Another money-saving trick is to offer to buy a round while people are still halfway through their drinks: some may wave you away, though others may line up glasses on the table. Trying to wriggle out of your round completely is not advised. The person who pleads an early night or another engagement just before his or her turn comes up is always noticed by the rest of the group. Once they've left, or even before, they will be roundly criticized by those present and forever after regarded as a "bludger" (sponger) who needs to be closely watched.

Occasionally someone will decide to shout a whole bar a drink. This is generally done by those who are (a) celebrating winning a lot of money, (b) so drunk they've lost their senses, or (c) in an empty bar.

On me

Beware: if you ask someone out for a drink in many parts of the world—India, Ghana, or Mexico, to name but three—the implication is that you will pay. Inviting someone out and then expecting them to pay for themselves would be considered the height of discourtesy.

Stammtisch

In rural pubs in the United Kingdom, you will occasionally find a particular chair reserved for George, Tom, or Maureen, a regular who appears every night at the same time and needs, for some reason, to sit in the same place. German pubs and *bierkellers* (beer halls) likewise often have a table set aside for regulars. This is called the *Stammtisch* and will usually be marked with a sign (or, in traditional beer halls, with a large brass plaque above the table). If you sit at *der Stammtisch* as an unwitting outsider, you will almost certainly be asked to move.

Tea total

In Saudi Arabia alcohol is illegal. Instead, as in the rest of the Arab world, you will be constantly offered tea and coffee. You should always accept, even if you take only a couple of sips. Generally you are offered tea first. When you've finished that, you'll be offered coffee. Then you'll be offered tea again, then more coffee. This process can go on for hours and is an important part of building relationships. As in Japan, you should never pour your own drink; wait for your cup to be filled. Likewise, it's up to you to refill your neighbor's cup or glass when it's half-empty.

Chaji

In Japanese homes and offices tea will often be offered informally. But should you ever be invited to a "tea ceremony," prepare yourself for something entirely different. The *chaji* is a highly formalized event, closer perhaps to a religious service than a tea party; the full four- or five-hour ceremony follows a mass of rules and rituals, which devotees can spend years perfecting.

If you attend such an occasion, be sure to wear clean socks and loose clothes. In addition to removing your shoes, you may be asked to change into a kimono; if not, after a few minutes in the ritual squat known as the *seiza,* you may regret wearing tight trousers. If the host notices his guests' private agony and asks them to make themselves comfortable, a man should move to a cross-legged position and a woman to one with legs tucked to one side. Never spread your legs straight out in front of you.

Some tea ceremonies begin with a light meal—or *kaiseki*—served on a tray with brand-new cedarwood chopsticks. If not, once you have entered through the small sliding door into the dedicated tea room—or *chashitsu*—and been seated on the *tatami,* you will be offered a small sweet cake, called *okashi.* You should eat it in several small bites, making sure all crumbs fall on the plate, not on you—or worse, the *tatami.*

After the host has ritually washed and dried the tea-making equipment, tea will be made. The host passes the tea bowl to the main guest, who bows in accepting it, before bowing to those guests who've not yet been served. The bowl is raised and rotated half a turn clockwise in the hand. The guest admires it before drinking, then drinks some of the tea, wipes the rim of the bowl, and passes it to the next guest.

The essence of the tea ceremony is the Zen-like harmony that is created by the formulaic ritual. Conversation should be kept to a polite minimum and God forbid that anyone should produce a business card.

The happiness of life

The Japanese are not the only ones with a formal approach to tea. In Mauritania and Niger tea is served in a three-part ceremony: first, a small cup without sugar, representing the hardness of life; then a second cup, with mint and sugar, reflecting how life improves once you get married; finally a very sweet cup, symbolizing the happiness of life when you have children. It's rude to leave before drinking all three cups.

Mate

In Argentina, Uruguay, Paraguay, and southern Brazil *mate* (pronounced ma-tey) is the beverage of choice. A bitter, mildly stimulating tea, *mate* is made from an infusion of dried leaves of the *yerba mate* plant in boiling water, which is carried in a gourd. It's a common sight in Montevideo to see people carrying their *mate* supplies around with them in a leather case, with space for a thermos, a gourd, and ample supplies of tea. The tea is sucked from the gourd through a six-inch-long metal straw—a *bombilla*. When passed the gourd, you should drink the whole thing before passing it back to the *cebador* (server) who will refill it with water and pass it on.

Ch'a

The origins of tea as a drink are the subject of unreliable myth. But ch'a was certainly popular in China many centuries before it was even heard of in the West, and was established as the national drink under the Tang dynasty (618–907 CE). Tea was first drunk in Europe by the Dutch, in the early seventeenth century—then a costly drink for the well-to-do.

The popularity of tea in the United Kingdom owes a lot to Catherine of Braganza, the Portuguese queen consort of Charles II. When she arrived in England in 1662, tea was so unknown that when she asked for a cup of it, they had to bring her a glass of beer instead. But because of her example, tea soon became popular at court and was then adopted as a smart drink by the aristocracy: exotic, high-priced, and heavily taxed.

Sea Cucumber and Reindeer Tongue

THE MEAL

The good news is that in the very act of sitting down to eat with someone of another culture you are being accepted and are on the way to some serious bonding. The bad news is that the path to this social nirvana is littered with hurdles, from *amuse-bouche* to *Birkat ha-Mazon*. . . .

Am I the first?

If you're invited to dinner at 7:00 p.m. in Germany, that means 7:00 p.m.; anything after 7:15 and you'll be thought impolite, even if the invite is for the light cold-cuts collation they call *Abendbrot* (evening bread) as opposed to the more substantial *Abendessen* (evening meal), which may also be eaten out in a restaurant. In France, you may stretch the *quart d'heure académique* a little, but don't be so late that you miss any of your hostess's carefully orchestrated series of courses. In Latin America, unless you want to catch your hosts in their curlers, it's not just fashionable but essential to be unpunctual. Turning up to dinner right on time in Argentina implies that you're over-keen to be at table—greedy, in fact. The same is true in Singapore.

When's dinner?

The world eats, in any case, at very different times. Poles breakfast well and early, then often have nothing till *obiad* between 2 and 4 p.m. Japanese salarymen may scoff a bowl of noodles at lunchtime, but they'll be hungry by 5 or 6 p.m. and ready for something more substantial (though those with a long commute may not get to eat till nine). Americans who still sit down together have their dinner early, around 6 or 6:30 p.m., while most Europeans wait till 7:30 or 8 p.m. Spanish, Portuguese, and Latin Americans enjoy a late lunch, so won't be ready for another big meal till much later; if you're asked for 8 p.m. dinner in Brazil, beware—you probably won't see a main course till 10 or 11 p.m., if not later.

RIP, RSVP

RSVPs are treated more casually these days, with consequent anxiety for hosts the world over. This is nothing new in Indonesia, where people have never been overeager to commit themselves to a social event, even if sent a written invitation with "RSVP" at the bottom. So if you're planning a party in Jakarta and want a good turnout, it's always best to follow up with a reminder. You may then have to divulge (a) what the party is celebrating, (b) who's coming, and (c) the name of the most important guest before people will deign to attend. Bear in mind that, as in other Asian cultures, people have a problem saying no, so a "Yes, I think I can make it" is absolutely no guarantee that they will appear.

My wife invites . . .

In Arab countries women rarely go out socially. If you invite a man and his wife (even to your home), the wife may well not turn up. The best plan, when trying to get a couple to come to dinner, is to use the formula "My wife invites your wife," while at the same time volunteering information about the other guests you're expecting. This will help the husband decide whether he wants his wife to meet these people, while assuring him that other women will be present, too.

Just sit anywhere

Though Western lunch or dinner parties these days often do without the old-fashioned formalities of placement, in countries as different as Saudi Arabia and South Korea seating arrangements are crucial, reflecting the status of individuals in the group and the honor being accorded to different guests.

Traditionally, in the United Kingdom and the United States, with both men and women present, the most important guests were placed to their opposite-gender host's right. So the most important man would sit to the hostess's right, and the most important woman to the host's right. The second most important man sat to the hostess's left, and so on down to the center of the table, from where the least important could observe their fascinating betters and gossip about them with one another. In the countries of mainland Europe, by contrast, host and hostess were more likely to sit with the important guests at the sides of the table, leaving the *bout de table* for the least important. When you do find placement these days, it's likely to at least pay homage to these traditions.

In China, the formal business dinner—or banquet—is likely to be an all-male affair, and usually at a round, rather than a rectangular, table. The leader of the group of guests will be placed in the seat of honor to the right of the host, facing the door, with the second most important guest to the right of the host's number two, at the opposite side of the table. The rest of the party will now be placed alternately, host then guest, in descending order of importance, with the bizarre result that the least important guest ends up on the other side of the host.

God's neat, let's eat

Before you sit to eat, in many cultures, some sort of prayer—or grace—may be said. In Muslim countries, it's pretty much universal to say *Bismillah* ("In the name of God") before tucking in. Practicing Jews say the *ha-Motzi* (known colloquially as "the *motzi*"), if not daily, then definitely before Friday night supper, when *Shabbat* (Sabbath) candles are lit, wine is sanctified, and special sweet braided egg-bread (*challah*) is eaten: "Blessed are You, Lord our God, King of the Universe, who brings forth bread from the earth." This is generally said in Hebrew, often by one of the younger children present. More observant Jews may ritually wash their hands first, which will be done in silence. Conversation begins again once the *motzi* is finished.

In American Christian households grace can vary from a prolonged "Bless us, O Lord and these thy servants . . ." to something altogether zippier: "Good food, good meat, good God,

let's eat"; "Please bless these sinners as they eat their dinners";
or even "God's neat, let's eat!"

Offering joy

Buddhist and Hindu prayers before food, by contrast, are more likely to put the emphasis on celebrating the oneness of existence or improving the spiritual condition of the humble humans gathered round the table:

With the first taste, I promise to offer joy.
With the second, I promise to relieve the suffering of others.
With the third, I promise to see others' joy as my own.
With the fourth, I promise to learn the way of nonattachment and
   equanimity.

Good appetite

Once seated, and before you actually put knife, fork, chopstick, or hand to your nosh, it's generally best to wait until the host or hostess has sat down with a full plate in front of them—or at least encouraged you to start. At this point yet more words may be said: *Bon Appétit!* in France, or *Sahtain!* in Arab countries, for example, while many Germans won't begin until the host has said *Guten Appetit!* In Argentina, likewise, they wait for the host to say *¡Buen provecho!* before tucking in. In Japan they say *Itadakimasu* ("I receive this gift thankfully"), while in China it's *Youyi!* ("Here's to friendship!").

Oshibori

In Japan, before you eat, you will often be offered a hot towel known as an *oshibori*. You use this to clean your hands, not your face or neck. And *never* blow your nose on it.

Excuse fingers

In countries where you are not offered a knife, fork, spoon, or chopsticks you will be expected to eat with your hands. In general—and certainly in the East—the right hand is used for eating, the left being reserved for a related function a few hours later. It is a serious social no-no to eat with the "unclean" hand.

In Africa you may be offered a communal bowl of food, and the left hand should be kept well away from that at all times. Some Africans have a custom of dipping their right index finger into the food first to taste it; this comes from an old habit of making sure the food is fresh and safe to eat. And eat only from that part of the bowl which is directly in front of you.

Despite having cutlery, certain hard-to-handle foods in the West are still eaten with fingers, at even the smartest tables; in the United States and United Kingdom these include asparagus, corn on the cob, crab, and spare ribs, while many consider it perfectly polite to pick up with either hand the nearly clean bone of a chicken leg or wing and gnaw it *à table*. In France there's a fine old custom of cleaning up the gravy on your plate with a spare piece of bread, while in Spain it's OK to take a prawn in your fingers. In Mexico, where *tacos* and *tortas* are eaten with both hands, it would be seen as actively snobbish to use a knife and fork.

Stalin's spoons

On BBC radio, Hugh Lunghi, British interpreter at Winston Churchill's wartime meetings with Stalin, recalled a dinner where he witnessed the Soviet tyrant seriously confused by the cutlery laid out in rows on either side of his plate. "How does one use these tools?" he asked. Once Lunghi had obliged with a demonstration, Stalin thanked him. "We are primitive in our approach to food," he said. "We have a lot to learn from you."

In Finland, however, you rarely eat anything with your fingers. In company, even an apple may be speared with a fork and peeled with a knife.

Uncle's privilege

Once upon a time in the leafy shires of England, traditionally minded nannies would seize the elbows of children that rested on the table with the words "All joints on the table are meant to be *carved*." The rough idea was that you weren't allowed to put your elbows on the table until (a) you had reached the age of twenty-one, or (b) you were an uncle. But in other countries, having nephews or nieces is no qualification for such barbarity. Americans find elbows on the table bad manners at all times, while the French like to see diners with straight backs and wrists resting gently on the table's edge.

Breaking bread

Estonians and Italians regard cutting bread with a knife as bad manners; it should be torn with the hands. The Italians also break off a corner of their bread before spreading it with butter, jam, anchovy paste, or whatever. Covering a whole slice of bread with jam and then biting from it is seen as rather gross.

Waribashi

Not every Asian country uses chopsticks; in Thailand they eat with a spoon and fork. But in Japan, China, Taiwan, Korea, and Vietnam chopsticks are the norm, and you should learn in advance the right way to use them. It's not exactly a faux pas to ask for Western cutlery, but many restaurants simply don't have such utensils available, so this is one area where it's worth getting up to speed.

Chopsticks should be held two-thirds up, with the sharp end

pointing toward the food (the farther away your fingers are from the bowl, in fact, the more sophisticated you are deemed to be). The lower chopstick is held stationary between the smaller two fingers and the base of forefinger and thumb. The upper chopstick is held between the top of the thumb and the fore and second finger, and moves, pincerlike, to pick up the food.

You should never spear food with your chopsticks, cross them over each other, rest them on opposite sides of your plate, point at people with them, use them to pull your bowl closer, wave them idly around the food, or—worst of all—stick them upright in a bowl of rice. This last is done only at funerals, when bowls of rice with upright chopsticks are placed on the altar of the deceased. Nor should you ever pass food with chopsticks. This, too, mimics a Japanese funeral rite—that of passing the bones of a cremated body from person to person.

When you eat in a restaurant in Japan, you will probably be offered *waribashi*, or disposable wooden chopsticks. Once you've removed them from their paper sleeve, you can impress your hosts by doing the local thing and turning that sleeve into a rest for your chopsticks. Fold it in half end-to-end, then tie the resultant strip of paper into a knot; on this you rest the blunt end of your sticks. *Waribashi* usually come joined at the top. You should separate them over your lap, making sure to keep any little splinters away from your food. When you've finished your meal, untie your knotted paper holder and put your used chopsticks back in their case; this tells your waiter that you've finished.

You should eat everything with chopsticks, down to the last grain of rice in your bowl. For soup, take out the pieces of food one by one, then drink the remaining liquid from the bowl. The only exception is *sushi,* which may be eaten with your hands. Dip only the top, fishy side into the soy sauce; if you try it with the rice side down, it will crumble apart and make a most undignified mess. And be careful not to mistake the sharp, green *wasabi* paste for *guacamole,* an all-too common mistake that will have you reaching in a hurry for the green tea.

wan, where your tools will usually be round, non-disposable, harder to handle, and won't come in a paper case. If you're not given a ceramic chopstick rest, you should put the food end of your chopsticks by your plate, not touching the table (in Korea and Vietnam likewise). And, if there's something in your mouth you want to remove—a piece of gristle or whatever—use the chopsticks or the porcelain soup spoon, rather than your fingers. Perversely, spitting it out on a side plate is fine.

Sushi and Sashimi

Sushi, *though widely used in the West to describe all Japanese snacks involving raw fish, refers in Japan to the vinegar-flavored rice served with fish, shellfish, seaweed, or other vegetables.* Sashimi *is a separate dish: the raw fish by itself—a cuisine that dates back to 123 CE, when the reigning emperor was served raw bonito and clams with vinegar by his head chef. By the mid-seventeenth century sea bass, red snapper, shark, eel, perch, carp, shellfish, and even meats such as pheasant and duck were used for sashimi, which was at that time still served with seasoned vinegar, not soy sauce as today.*

Soy no-no

Pouring soy sauce onto rice—much done in the West—is a total no-no in Japan. Quite apart from the fact that rice is sacred, soy spoils the delicate flavor that you should be savoring.

Slippery

In both China and Korea it's standard to use toothpicks between courses. At the table you use the toothpick with one hand while covering your mouth with the other; it's not polite to show the open mouth or teeth. It's also considered OK to use a toothpick to spear very slippery pieces of food—jellyfish, button mushrooms, and the like—that you can't hold with chopsticks.

And if you want more tea, there's no need to pester the waiters; just turn your empty cup upside down in its saucer and they'll bring you a fresh one. If you have an empty pot, turn the lid upside down and balance it on the handle for a refill.

Goat's eye and rat cake

If at some point during a meal you are offered "the local delicacy," it's important to accept, even if it makes you sick to your back teeth just to look at the baleful goat's eye on your plate. Bear's paw soup in China, cat or dog stew in Korea, rat pudding in Arunachal Pradesh—to be offered such dishes is always a rare honor, if not an important sign of acceptance. If you really can't manage to get the delicacy down your gullet, you must at least acknowledge the honor. One way out is to say, with great politeness, that while you enormously appreciate the honor (in your heart), you would prefer to grant it to (the belly of) another who would value it just as much. Then pass the dish.

Global delights

These are some of the more challenging foods and delicacies you may be offered if things are going well with you and your hosts:

(Aboriginal) Australia	witchetty grubs
Bali	charcoal-roasted or boiled dragonfly
China	"sea cucumber" (slugs), bird's nest soup, goat's penis soup, bear's paw soup, "dragon and tiger and phoenix" (snake, cat, and chicken stew),

74

bullfrog, chicken feet, "hundred-year-old" eggs, donkey stew

Ethiopia	fresh blood, fried coagulated blood
Ethiopia	fresh blood, fried coagulated blood
France	pig's trotters and intestines, cow's stomach, lamb's brains, snails, horsemeat
Hong Kong	chicken feet, turkey testicles (an aphrodisiac, supposedly)
Japan	*sashimi* (raw fish), *fugu* (poisonous blowfish), *uni* (sea urchin roe—another alleged aphrodisiac), *inago* (fried grasshopper), *semi* (fried cicada), *sangi* (fried silk moth pupae), *hachi-no-ko* (boiled wasp larvae), *natto* (fermented soya beans with strong smell of ammonia)
Malaysia	durian fruit
Mexico	chocolate-coated ants
Nigeria	*kanni* (a caterpillar), palm weevil larvae, compost beetle larvae
Philippines	*balut* (a duck egg containing a gestating embryo)
Scotland	haggis (sheep's heart, lung, and liver, mixed with oatmeal, and boiled in its stomach bag)
Siberia	raw reindeer liver or meat, reindeer blood
South America	deep-fried guinea pig
South Korea	cat or dog stew
Spain	*calamares en su tinta* (squid in their own ink)
Thailand	crocodile fillets with mustard sauce, cobra with bamboo worms, mountain frog
Tuscany	boiled cow's stomach
Vietnam	armadillo steak, coffee brewed from beans vomited by weasels

This last is not a joke. The resulting drink has a stronger and smoother taste than normal coffee and is exceeded in rarity only by the Indonesian coffee made from beans that have been half-digested (and excreted) by the Sumatran civet cat.

Sheep's eyes

British diplomats have generally at some point in their careers had to put country before regurgitation reflex and stomach the "local delicacy." Michael Shea, former press secretary to the Queen, recalled in a BBC radio program eating rat in South America and dried bat in the Pacific Islands. "You have to be polite about it because it can be one of the national dishes," he told listeners. In a similar line of duty, seasoned Middle Eastern diplomat Sir Antony Acland had experienced the famous "sheep's head ceremony," where the eyeball is given to the guest of honor. "You knew that honor was being done to you and the host knew he was doing honor to you," he remembered. "But it wasn't exactly a tasty morsel."

Separate sinks

In a life dedicated to God, the devout Jew is allowed to eat only food that is *kosher*. This includes all fruit and vegetables and any animal that has both "a completely split hoof and chews the cud" (Leviticus 11:3). This includes cows, sheep, and goats but rules out pigs, horses, camels, and rabbits. As for birds, turkey, duck, chicken, goose, pheasant, and pigeon are in; eagles, ravens, cormorants, owls, and many other birds of prey are out. Fish with detachable fins and scales are *kosher;* crab, shellfish, eel, and octopus are *treyfah*—forbidden. Continuing debate surrounds certain indeterminate fish, such as turbot and monkfish, which don't have proper scales.

Following the verse "You must not cook a young goat in its mother's milk" (Exodus 23:19), Jews who keep *kosher* kitchens do not mix meat and dairy products. They often have entirely separate sets of crockery, cutlery, and cooking utensils for meat and dairy, and in Orthodox homes these will be washed in separate sinks and kept in separate cupboards. A wait of between three and six hours is generally observed between meat and dairy, though in some places this can be less (fifty-five minutes in the Netherlands). *Pareve* foods (anything not meat or dairy, such as fruit and vegetables) may be eaten with either meat or dairy—a relatively recent addition to the *kosher* table is *pareve* ice cream, made without milk products, which can be eaten after a meat meal. If you are visiting a *kosher* household, remember not to ask for butter to go with bread during a meal containing meat, or milk for coffee afterward.

Halal and *haram*

Muslims have similarly strict rules about the food they may eat, which are laid down in the Koran: *halal* (permitted), as opposed to *haram* (forbidden). *Haram* foods include pork and all its by-products, such as lard or gelatines; blood; alcohol and food containing alcoholic extracts; and animals that have died a natural death or been killed for reasons other than food. Animals intended for food have to be slaughtered in a certain ritual way, by a Muslim.

Uzooma

In Arab countries you will always be offered more food when you've emptied your plate. You will be asked to take more two or three times, in a ritual known as the *uzooma*. You should refuse the first time; the host will insist and you should refuse again; the host will insist again and then you should give in. If you really don't want more, leave something on your plate.

In Belgium, likewise, leaving a bit of food means that you've had enough. In Thailand, too, it's a positive sign—thank you, I've enjoyed my meal. But in the United Kingdom or North America, where children are taught to "clean their plates," leftovers are regarded as a little uncouth; and in El Salvador, where so many live on the breadline, leaving any food at all is seen as wasteful, if not wrong.

The sound of silence

The French have a phrase for that moment during a dinner party when all conversations suddenly cease at once and there is silence before a new topic is begun—*un ange passe* (an angel passes)—perhaps because a lively conversation around the table is their ideal. But in many other cultures silence when eating is acceptable or even required. The Chinese and Japanese don't necessarily expect to talk while eating, nor do Finns or Ugandans.

宴会

The number one eating-out experience in China is the *yan hui* (宴会), or banquet, which is likely to be part of any even moderately successful business trip. Though your host will never expect you to know every last nicety of correct behavior, he is certain to be delighted if you understand the basics.

Banquets are usually held in the special private rooms of restaurants. If you are in a group, all members should arrive together and on time. This may be early: 6 or 6:30 p.m. You will be met at the door and led to the banquet room, where your hosts will be waiting for you. The most important person in your group should go in first. Your hosts may well greet you by clapping as you enter; the polite thing to do is not to smile and nod bemusedly but to clap back. Then shake hands with everyone

You will now be seated, one by one, in order of importance (see page 68).

The banquet begins with the host offering food to the most important guest. Either that, or he'll raise his chopsticks to announce that the meal has started. Now you may serve yourself as much food as you like, though go carefully, as there may be up to fifteen courses, and to stop eating in the middle of a banquet is regarded as bad manners.

Traditionally, the feast starts with cold, sweet appetizers and moves on through soup and steamed vegetables, seafood, and meat courses to the *pièce de résistance:* a whole fish, served with head, skin, and fins (it's considered bad luck to turn the fish over to get at the flesh under the bones). After this comes more soup, then fruit or a dessert. Right at the end comes the *fan,* or bowl of rice, which should only be picked at to indicate that you can eat no more. Feel free to compliment your hosts on the quality of the food as often as you like throughout the meal—it's almost impossible to overdo the politeness.

Toasting is an important part of the banquet, and will be started by the host. He will hold out his glass—usually filled with *maotai,* a 65 to 70 percent proof liquor made from fermented sorghum—with both hands and say a few words, sometimes apologizing for the meagerness of the meal to follow, and concluding with *Ganbei!* All follow suit, draining their glasses, and tipping them toward the host to show that they've drunk. After this, it's open season on both drinking and toasting, which may be made person to person or to the group as a whole, though you must remember, as always in the East, (a) never to fill your own glass, and (b) when you drink spirits or *maotai,* as opposed to wine, beer, or soft drinks, it must be as part of a toast. A good host is honor-bound to try and get his guests drunk. Pleasantly so, as of course falling over or throwing up would mean loss of face.

When the last dish has been eaten, the meal ends without ceremony. The host will stand and announce that it was his pleasure to invite everyone to the banquet. This is the signal for everyone to stumble out to their cars—if, that is, they can still fit through the door. The host will go with them to see them off; should you be the host, you should do the same.

The famous Arab belch

Making a noise while eating is generally considered rude in the West. Masticating loudly, slurping soup or, God forbid, burping are all things that are frowned on in European cultures. In the Far East, however, loud guzzling of noodles or soup is not just considered OK, it's essential. Slurping, it's said, cools off noodles and enhances the flavor, and is a compliment to the chef.

There's a long-standing Western myth that Arabs like to belch loudly after a meal to show their appreciation to the host and/or cook. Some Americans also believe this to be true of the French and Germans. But this is, in fact, more of a north and central African custom (you'll find it in countries such as Kenya and Nigeria), and the belch should only be small. In China, too, a little burpette, as part of the post-slurping, "aaaaah" routine that indicates you've enjoyed your meal, is more than acceptable.

Dayman

What *is* expected, though, in Arab countries as elsewhere, is an expression of thanks. At the end of the meal guests should praise the food they've eaten and say *Dayman* ("always," as in "May there always be plenty at your table") or *Alhamdu lillah* ("Thanks be to God"). Similar expressions are repeated around the world. The Bangladeshi version is *Sukhur ethamdulillah*, while the Japanese say *Gochisosama deshita*. Jews have a complete grace to be said after meals, should they wish—the *Birkat ha-Mazon*—and, in contrast to the *ha-Motzi,* the honor of leading is sometimes given to a guest.

Traditionally, this grace included the phrase "I've never overlooked a righteous man who was destitute, with his children begging for bread." After the horrors of the Holocaust some progressive Jews have replaced this with a prayer that reflects the limits of God's powers: "May we not be blind to the needs of others, nor deaf to their cry for food. . . . Help us remove hunger and want from the world."

Glorious flowers

Be wary of being too effusive with your compliments to well-off people in countries such as India or the Philippines, where the meal will almost certainly have been prepared by the cook. Try instead to find something personal to praise. That lovely floral centerpiece, for example, is more likely to have been something that your hostess has managed to put together herself.

Doggy bag and *pabaon*

In the United States there is a tradition of taking home restaurant food that isn't finished at table in a "doggy bag" or "to-go box." Though originally the idea was that the scraps were for the pet left at home, now it's generally accepted that leftovers will be reheated in the microwave and eaten by humans the next day. Americans are completely at ease with this custom and are likely to cite the starving in the Third World to any visiting Europeans who try to tell them that lugging cold food home for later consumption is gross.

A similar custom in the Philippines, known as *pabaon,* applies to meals in private homes, where leftover food is given to guests to take away. In Samoa, likewise, if you attend a wedding or other celebratory meal, you'll be given a big box of food for all the relatives who couldn't come with you.

Garçon!

There is practically nowhere in the world where summoning waiters with a whistle or a click of the fingers is acceptable. Try it, and they will find ways of making you suffer—especially if you order the soup. In most places a discreet wave will do the trick, perhaps accompanied by a smile and suitably imploring eyes.

All the beckoning no-nos described earlier apply equally at the table. In Indonesia, such a gesture should be done with a very slight movement of all four fingers, palm down. In China it's best just to use eye contact. An exception to all this pussy-footedness is good old-fashioned Yemen, where you may clap your hands twice to summon staff.

Tipping tips

As anyone who has tried to walk out of a restaurant in the United States without tipping knows, leaving extra money for the waitstaff is expected in America; you may well get shouted at or even chased down the street if you don't. Elsewhere the custom varies widely. At one end of the scale you have Italy, where you're expected to tip on top of an added service charge; at the other, Thailand, Japan, or New Zealand, where the practice is uncommon and a tip will generally be refused. In Japan they may do the opposite of the United States and chase you down the street if you *do* leave money on the table. The most tip-averse country in the world is Iceland, where paying more than the service charge is seen as an insult.

Going Dutch in Beijing

In cultures that put emphasis on, if not social equality, then at least equality while socializing, splitting the bill after a meal out in a restaurant—"going Dutch" as the English say—is common. So you'll find diners divvying up bills in Scandinavia, the

Netherlands, the United Kingdom, Australia, and the United States—sometimes to a point beyond tedium. Eating out with one of those killjoys who insist on totting up in detail everyone's individual liability, one may cry out for the generosity of spirit of southern European, Middle Eastern, and Latin American cultures, where people *fight* to get the bill—and where the idea that Susie should pay less because she didn't have an appetizer or Roger more because he's enormous and drinks like a fish would not be understood or, if it were, would be considered embarrassing.

In South America, interestingly, the phrase for splitting the cost of a meal is *pagar a la Americana* (to pay American-style), while in Italy they say *pagare alla romana*, which is most unfair to the Romans, who are undoubtedly just as generous as the rest of their compatriots. In China the very concept of splitting the bill can be offensive. If you are invited out to a restaurant, your host will pay; you should politely demur and offer to pick up the tab yourself (up to three times), but to suggest a contribution would cause him or her to seriously lose face. Reciprocate at a later date with a splendid meal for which you fork out. No, unless you're out with young people, you should never even attempt to "go Dutch" in Beijing.

Happy birthday, everyone

In the United Kingdom people generally take the birthday girl or boy out for a meal and join together to pay for them. Elsewhere, it's often the opposite: it's your birthday, so you entertain your friends. At such a meal in the Netherlands you're expected to shake hands with everyone present and congratulate everyone related to the birthday person: children, for example, are congratulated on the birthday of their parents.

In China birthdays are not celebrated at all. Age is reckoned from the moment of conception, so a baby is already almost one when it's born. Instead, the seventh day of the Chinese New Year is celebrated as "everyone's birthday."

Onchi

Visitors to some households in the United Kingdom may be surprised when, rather than being allowed to sit quietly after dinner with their conversation and *digestifs,* they are co-opted into participatory games, ranging from word or name games such as Call My Bluff or Botticelli to full-on acting efforts such as Charades. In the East the postprandial entertainment of choice is most likely to be *karaoke,* and if you're invited along, you should try to have a song ready to sing—it really doesn't matter how well you perform it. In these countries where keeping "face" is normally so important, making a fool of yourself in an

---

Empty bucket

Karaoke *(empty bucket)** *is generally agreed to have originated in the Japanese city of Kobe in the 1970s. Prior to that, joining in with musical entertainment had always been popular in Japan, and one of the traditional requirements of a Japanese warrior—or* samurai—*was to have a song or dance he could perform at dinner. Though the Music Minus One label issued classical and jazz tracks without individual instruments and vocals as early as the 1950s in the United States, the invention of* karaoke *proper is credited to Japanese musician Daisuke Inoue, who in the early 1970s responded to requests for copies of his performances in piano and guitar bars by coming up with a tape recorder that played a song without vocals for one hundred yen. In a country famous for its public conformity this individualistic outlet soon became a fad, then a craze, then a worldwide sensation, with technology to match.*

---

* *Not* "empty orchestra" *as is frequently written.*

informal social context will make your hosts think you are a great sport. The Japanese, incidentally, refer to someone who sings out of tune as an *onchi*, while a particular song you do well is an *ohako*.

We really must be going

When you're offered an orange juice or other soft drink at the end of a French dinner party, it means it's time to leave. The same is true when iced water is brought out in the Middle East. There, when you say you're leaving, your hosts will encourage you to stay and tell you it's still early. This is purely a ritual offer. You shouldn't take it literally.

Holding Hands in the Temple

OUT AND ABOUT

It's not just the niceties of noshing that require thought. As you settle into your new country, you will find many everyday things done differently. Perhaps the hot tap in your hotel bedroom will be marked C (for *chaud, caldo,* or *caliente*) while the cold is marked F (for *froid, freddo,* or *frio*). Discovering that you're cleaning your teeth with warm water while your longed-for bath is stone cold will not be your only shock. Once you step out of the lobby onto the street, there'll be numerous other reasons why you may be surprised to the point of outrage. God forbid that that outrage should be directed at you. . . .

Nose shit

The Japanese do not use handkerchiefs as we do. They find the idea of holding on to *hanakuso* (nose shit) in a cloth in your pocket grotesque. Blowing your nose in public is also regarded as rude. If you must do it, turn away and use a disposable tissue, retreat to the toilet, or snort it back inside your body, as they do. Handkerchiefs are strictly for wiping your hands or mouth.

In general, it's best not to blow your nose in front of others right across the East, from Saudi Arabia, through China to Malaysia—especially at mealtimes.

Spitting is much more acceptable. In China people happily spit out bones on the tablecloth during meals; out and about, even on buses and trains, it's a free-for-all, particularly in rural areas.

Public display of affection

In Iran, Saudi Arabia, Egypt, or Thailand you may well see two men walking arm in arm or holding hands. This is nothing more than a sign of friendship. But for a woman and a man to do the same in the Arab world would be unthinkable—in Saudi Arabia it's illegal and punishable by flogging. Heterosexual couples visiting Gulf Arab countries should be aware of these strictures, as they apply to foreign nationals as well as natives.

In Thailand, however, nobody much minds what foreigners get up to; in rural areas *farangs* (foreigners) and their odd behavior are a source of continuing amusement to the locals.

Gasper

Smoking is generally on the retreat in Western society. Even at tables outside cafés and bars people often ask for permission to light up, something that would have been highly unlikely even five years ago. And it's now illegal to smoke inside a restaurant or bar in London, Dublin, and New York. Frustrated puffers are even denied their own private smoking zones and are forced out onto cold streets, where (in New York) the bar may be fined if they make too much noise.

Those who object to this healthification of public space should consider immigrating to the Middle East. In Arab countries, particularly those of the Levant and Maghreb, a man's right to smoke is still nonnegotiable. If you do see No Smoking signs in waiting rooms, elevators, and on trains, you will also see Arab men ignoring them. The only exception to this is dur-

---

Corrective

In Singapore the authorities have taken the control of public conduct to the extreme. Uncivilized behavior—from littering to not flushing public toilets—is illegal and attracts a big fine, followed by a Corrective Work Order (CWO) on a second offense. So you could be faced with a fine of up to S$1,000 (about US$700) for a first offense of littering, while a second could cost S$2,000 and see you working off your CWO picking up other people's trash for a day in a public park or on a beach. Offenders are made to feel their shame: they have to wear bright jackets, and the media may well be called to report the event.

Gum chewers beware: the import, sale, and possession of that confectionery is banned—you're not even allowed to bring in a small amount for personal consumption. As for drugs, the prohibition is total. The death penalty is mandatory for anyone convicted of trafficking or importing more than 15 grams of heroin, 30 grams of cocaine, 200 grams of cannabis resin, or 500 grams of cannabis, and possession is taken as prima facie evidence of trafficking.

ing the month of Ramadan, when smoking is forbidden between dawn and dusk. In China, too, smoking is still regarded as a right; indeed, as a rather *macho* habit. If another man offers you a cigarette at a meal or party, he'd expect you to take it.

Privy secrets

Visitors to Continental Europe should remember to always carry small change when they're likely to be caught short: using the restroom is often not free of charge. Those Sanisette booths that lurk like time machines on the streets of Paris cost €0.50 to access, and even toilets in bars and restaurants generally require a token from the waiter. The state of French toilets may also come as a shock, given the sophistication of the French in other areas. Even the plushest Parisian restaurant, which takes infinite trouble over food, wine, and service, may have a grim *toilette* out back (sometimes, still, just a basic hole in the floor).

Westerners traveling east of Istanbul should be aware that toilet paper is a rare commodity in some countries, where water from a bucket or nozzle and the left hand are often regarded as adequate cleaners of the nether regions. In Korea and many parts of China, if you are lucky enough to find toilet paper, you should not flush it down the drain, but throw into the wastebaskets provided (low water pressure and poor-quality paper means that drains are easily and often clogged). Footprints on the rim in Russia may cause surprise, but in a country where many toilet seats have been stolen, some Russians prefer to squat over the bowl.

In the souk

Some cultures have set prices for goods in their shops, and it would be regarded as strange to question them. In Great Britain, Germany, Portugal, and Chile, if that dress you want costs $90, it costs $90. You might offer less in a charity shop, but even that might bring a frown. But in such places as Mexico, Morocco, and Myanmar everything is up for grabs. There are no written prices, and the figure quoted by the shop or stall owner may be many times what he or she wants for it.

To get the result you want in the souk or at the stall you should take a deep breath and divide the quoted price by at least ten. So to buy that hand-embroidered Qarawiyyin *thobe* your charming Berber vendor is asking 400 *dirhams* for, you offer 40. This will be met immediately by a practiced look of astonishment, accompanied by remarks of the "What are you trying to do, rob me / send my mother to an early grave?" variety. But in fact your man will now respect you as a serious player, as you haggle back and forth until you reach the price he's after, generally somewhere between a quarter and a third of the asking price, say 130 *dirhams* tops. Walking off when he will drop no lower is also a good tactic; he'll almost certainly follow you and offer you an even better price. If he doesn't, then you know you've pushed him as far as he'll go. You can always call back later.

Bear in mind, too, that in haggling cultures it's good luck to be the first or last shopper at a stall. At the tourist-free markets of Myanmar the cries of "Lucky money, lucky money!" from stallholders who have yet to make a sale will follow you hauntingly as you walk away, your *kyats* still in your purse. If you do buy, they will bless their remaining goods by tapping your notes on them.

Shop horror

Offering your hard-earned money for merchandise is a very diverse experience around the world. In Russia retail assistants can sometimes be alarmingly abrupt, and in the United Kingdom, all too often, you may find yourself treated as an irritating interruption to the ongoing life and chitchat of the shop. In France the capital has a reputation for rudeness, but you'll get an altogether better level of service if you keep returning to the same place and join in with the whole rigmarole of *politesse*, saying *Bonjour m'sieur/madame*, replying in French, saying *Au revoir* when you leave, and so on. In Australia, despite—or perhaps because of—their nominal classlessness, retail workers seem very comfortable with the idea of service; as you browse, you will be asked, frequently, "Are you right?" (To which the answer is, "Yes, OK, just looking," rather than, "Right about *what* exactly?"). In Japan they are even more assiduous: you will be personally greeted as you enter and leave the shop—sometimes by a man standing on a stepladder with a megaphone. In Italy they will greet you with a friendly *Buongiorno,* fuss over you, and even offer to wrap up your purchase with paper and ribbons.

Road rage

Driving styles differ widely from country to country and are reflected interestingly in road accident statistics. In Sweden, one of the safer countries to take a car around, you must keep your lights on in daylight and avoid all alcohol whatsoever before taking to the road. In Germany be very careful what you drink—their driving-under-the-influence level of fifty milligrams per milliliter of blood can be reached after a single beer, and restrictions are strictly applied. In Italy they have a similarly low alcohol limit but, though you are less likely to be caught, you need to keep your reactions sharp; out on the *autostrada* drivers appear not to care whether they live or die: tailgating at high speeds is normal, passing on the inside lane likewise. In South America driving is even more hazardous. Red lights are treated more as a suggestion than as indicators to be obeyed; at night car lights are often left off—so as not to dazzle other drivers. Indeed, if you put on your lights, an angry driver may try and run you off the road.

The message is simple. If you want to avoid road rage when abroad, take a taxi.

Road accidents: number of people injured per 100,000 population per annum

1. Qatar	9,681
2. Kuwait	2,155
3. Rwanda	1,764
4. Costa Rica	1,438
5. Saudi Arabia	1,353
6. Panama	1,262
7. Jordan	1,023
8. Barbados	763
9. Japan	749
10. United States	704

Women drivers

In Saudi Arabia it's still illegal to drive a car if you are a woman. As recently as 2005 a statement warning against the dangers of allowing women to drive was released on the Internet. It was signed by more than a hundred sheikhs, imams, judges, Islamic scholars, and heads of Promotion of Virtue and Prevention of Vice centers in the kingdom.

Matey

Never open a taxi door in Japan. If the car doesn't have an automatic door, the driver will get out and open it for you. Once inside the vehicle, normal hierarchies continue to be observed. The most important person sits in the middle of the backseat, with subordinates to left and right.

In Australia, by contrast, it's traditional to demonstrate your general matiness by jumping into the front seat, alongside the driver. These days, though, as most taxi drivers in the big cities of Oz are Asian, this is increasingly a rural custom.

Toucans and jays

In the United Kingdom there are virtually no controls on pedestrian behavior. Though the Highway Code advises crossing the road using one of the imaginatively named zebra, pelican, toucan, or puffin crossings, this is not backed up by law. This is not the case in the United States and much of western Europe, where not waiting for the Walk sign or the little green man constitutes jaywalking and may land you with a substantial fine, or even, in the case of Singapore, in jail.

Stealing souls

Quite apart from anything else, a camera is a visible symbol of (relative) wealth. So if you take a photograph of a penniless Moroccan goatherd, don't be surprised if he asks you for money. There are parts of the world where the very poor have too much dignity to stoop to begging, but Morocco is not one of them. Nor is India.

In Germany it's considered rude to photograph strangers in public without their permission, but otherwise in the West, taking someone's picture is rarely regarded as an intrusion, unless you are a press photographer at an accident or a gate crasher at a private party of celebrities. This attitude doesn't apply worldwide. Some Aboriginal Australians, for example, believe that if you make an image of them you are stealing their souls, an idea also found among indigenous communities in the rainforests of the Amazon.

In most parts of the world, though, the "review" feature of a digital camera can make you instant friends. A machine that can catch a likeness immediately is a magic toy. Just be careful that behind the grinning faces in the foreground there are not others scowling and plotting to rid you of your technological advantage.

Aussie rules

Interest in sports is universal, so it pays to be aware of nation-grabbing events in specific areas, such as Wimbledon for tennis, the Tour de France for cycling, the U.S. Open for golf, or Manila's World Slasher Cup for cockfighting. But in Australia, sports come close to being the national religion. That Friday business meeting will be taken over for a good half hour with a long discussion of the upcoming Aussie Rules game—and when cricket's on, you can forget any other conversation for the duration, certainly among the fellers.

If you're male, Australians will assume that, de facto, you share their passion. And not just for their teams and leagues, but yours too. They may very likely be more up to speed on your national sports than you are, and assume that you'll know the names and histories of key players. As with all religions, this sacred activity is not to be mocked.

Sweating it out

Taking a sauna comes close to being the Finnish national pastime. In a population of five million there are more than two million saunas, many of them still the traditional smoke-heated *savusauna*, which provides the ultimate mutual sweating experience. If invited to a sauna, even by a business contact you don't know well, accept: taking a sauna may be a way of working through a difficult negotiating point or even celebrating a successful deal. You will sit in the nude beside each other, but this has no hint of the sexual about it—in Finland whole families sauna together naked.

You should always shower before stepping into the sauna. Take a towel with you, and sit on it (we needn't go into details of why it's unhygienic not to). Sit where you want: there's no *macho* requirement to sweat it out on the hotter upper shelves— taking a sauna is about relaxing, not competing. In addition to sitting naked, some Finns take birch branches in with them and gently flagellate themselves. Don't look askance: this is not some weird masochistic activity but a sensible way of opening up pores. In more old-fashioned saunas, you may be surprised to find yourself being offered a body scrub by a resident washer-woman. Accept graciously: this is a fine old Finnish custom, however painful it turns out to be when her gristly fingers actually get to work on your shoulders. In winter there may be an invitation to roll in the snow outside or even jump through an ice hole into a frozen lake afterward. Clearly it would be churlish to refuse these invigorating traditional delights.

In the temple

Obviously you should always be respectful in holy buildings. This means shoes off for everyone in mosques and Hindu and Buddhist temples, while Western women should cover up exposed flesh—not only here but in Christian churches, too. Most well-visited Christian sites now have shawls or paper capes on hand for those who've got bare arms, low-cut tops, or shorts. But in a mosque a woman would be expected to be wearing a head covering, a long-sleeved blouse, and loose-fitting pants at the very least before entering. Before stepping inside a Shinto shrine in Japan you should wash both hands and mouth. And remember: it's traditional to walk clockwise around a Buddhist temple, both inside and out.

Few religions object to outsiders observing a service, provided they do so quietly and reverently. Wandering around in shorts and/or filming worshipers with your video camera is clearly not OK. When it comes to participation, attitudes vary: visitors to Mahayana Buddhist temples are actively encouraged to participate in rituals, particularly that of buying an incense stick and holding it at face level to make a wish or a prayer before entering the temple proper, while Christians who turn to each other before the Eucharist, shake hands, and say "Peace be with you" will be delighted if an outsider joins in. But Muslims would not expect visitors to a mosque to prostrate themselves on the carpet in the direction of Mecca any more than Christians would expect outsiders to take part in Commu-

---

Uncommon eras

Ethiopians follow the Coptic calendar, which has twelve months of thirty days, and a thirteenth short month of five or six days; this results in a seven-year difference between the Coptic and Gregorian (Western) calendars. Business typically follows the Gregorian calendar. The year begins on September 11, with the month of Tout, providing a pause for thought for conspiracy theorists.

In Israel the initials CE after a year stand for Common Era and are the equivalent of the Gregorian AD (Anno Domini— "in the year of our Lord"). The separate Jewish calendar has its own months and years and is calculated by adding 3760 to the civil (Gregorian) year—this figure was originally arrived at by adding together the ages of people mentioned in the Old Testament back to the time of Creation. So 2008 CE will be 5768 in Hebrew years.

The Islamic calendar is more recent: it starts with the Prophet's Hegira (emigration) from Mecca to Medina in AD 622. Hegira dates are marked AH (Anno Hegirae): subtract 622 years and add AH (2008 CE is 1386 AH). The Islamic year is divided into twelve lunar months, which average twenty-nine and a half days, making it eleven days shorter than the Western year, so Muslim festivals and holidays fall on earlier dates every year. Ramadan, which began on March 16 in 1991, will start on September 2 in 2008.

nion. (Roman Catholics are particularly strict in this regard. With the exception of special ecumenical services, they don't allow Protestants to share their sacrament of bread and wine.)

Financial offerings always go over well in religious places: a note in the collection plate in church or *tzedakah* (charity) box in a synagogue, or some coins for the old gentleman whose job it is to look after the buddhas in a temple, will usually bring a smile.

The Lord's Day

The Jewish Sabbath—*Shabbat*—runs from sunset on Friday to sunset on Saturday. During *Shabbat* buses and trains in Israel do not operate, nor does El Al, the national airline (though Ben-Gurion International Airport in Tel Aviv does). The roads of religious neighborhoods are empty of cars, though traffic can be heavy in secular areas. Orthodox Jews do not cook, write, sew, dig in the garden, or answer the phone, and even with the less observant you should ask if it's all right to call. Two *Shabbat* candles are lit and even these should remain "work-free"—you shouldn't use them to light another candle because that's making them work.

Equally stern strictures about the holy day off are observed in the remote Scottish islands of the northern Hebrides, home to the several theologically differing sects of the Free Church of Scotland (known locally as the "Wee Frees"). One thing, however, they all agree on: to do anything at all on the Lord's Day of Sunday is wrong. Pubs, shops, and garages are closed. There's no public transportation. Even swings in the children's playground are padlocked.

Jeitinho and Nyekulturny

CUSTOMS AND ATTITUDES

Some attitudes go deeper than the kind of thing that can be explained or prohibited by a sign on the wall. As you watch everyone barging past you and helping themselves to the best treats from the buffet; as you hand over a few rupees to a beggar and are surrounded by a horde demanding the same treatment for them; as you look through your taxi window at the remote district your taxi driver has brought you to and realize he was being highly economical with the truth when he said he knew where your hotel was—you could be excused for harboring feelings of confusion, if not resentment. But you have only yourself to blame. All these situations are the result of entirely understandable cultural differences. As the visitor, it's your call to do the understanding. . . .

Lines are generally religiously observed in the United Kingdom, Australia, New Zealand, Sweden, and other Nordic countries, where "cutting in" for any reason at all is completely unacceptable, with an almost moral dimension to the objection. However discreetly you try and get ahead, you will be noticed by people farther down the line, who will start to mutter threateningly. If you persist and refuse to wait your turn, you may be shouted at or even physically manhandled.

A more informal system exists in countries such as Spain and Israel. People don't line up, but they know exactly who's next, rather as Britons do at the bar of a pub. So if you arrive at a stall in a Spanish market, you should ask who the last person waiting is, then keep an eye on them until they're served. In Cuba they shout out *¿El último?* ("Who's last?").

But in places as different as Italy, the Middle East, and South Korea lining up just doesn't happen. Nobody waits in turn for a buffet in Italy, for example. They'll pile in and help themselves from the dishes they want, resulting, they would say, in everyone getting served quicker. This impatience about waiting is perhaps most surprising in Germany, where public behavior is otherwise extremely orderly, with men opening doors for women, younger people walking closer to the curb than older, and signs that read *Geschlossen* (Closed), *Kein Zutritt* (No Entry), *Ruhe* (Silence), and *Nicht Rauchen* (No Smoking) treated with respect.

Some more equal

In Communist Russia the masses had to wait for everything— and they hated it, especially because party officials and anyone important would jump the line, ushered by some crawling *apparatchik,* or just march up to the front knowing nobody would dare stop them. In these more democratic times things are fairer. Some self-important Russians may try to skip the line, but they are far more likely to be challenged, and occasionally they'll be shamed back into place. More often they'll press ahead, lips pursed, feigning deafness. As a visitor, you should of course join the line—unless you're in the company of a very powerful oligarch with a couple of bodyguards.

About face

Protecting "face"—or the dignity of yourself and others—is central throughout the Middle and Far East. Losing your temper at a meeting or in public, for example, is a shameful loss of face; if you do this in Asia, you'll be neither trusted nor respected. Being confrontational, insulting people, calling attention to someone's error, or otherwise creating embarrassment will all result in a loss of face—for both you and your counterpart. In short, you should never do anything in the East that makes you or anyone else look foolish.

On a trivial level this can lead to some comic extremes. If you're out in a bar in South Korea with a group of business associates and buy a particular brand of beer, you may find that all those with you will do the same, so there's absolutely no danger of you "losing face" over your choice. The trick here is to let them have one round the same as you before graciously suggesting that everyone should choose their own brand.

I'll think about it

Often for reasons of "face" many Eastern cultures find it hard to say no. In Japan, for example, the best face must always be put on the worst situation, so if this means not offending someone by not saying no, then so be it—whatever confusion may result. Tales of Tokyo taxi drivers telling their foreign customers they know where they're going when they have no idea are sadly all too true.

100   "That may be difficult," "I'll think about it," "I will seriously

consider it," "I'll give it my utmost consideration"—in Japan all these expressions mean no, as does the almost silent sucking of breath through the teeth. And the Japanese word *hai* (yes) is more likely to mean "I'm listening, keep talking" than "I agree with everything you say."

The same applies in Thailand. People may make unlikely excuses, pretend that they don't understand English, or even invent a nonexistent superior they have to "check with" in order to avoid saying no. In Indonesia things are even worse: the Bahasa language has no fewer than twelve ways of saying yes but meaning no.

"The Asiatic"

"In official dealings, while it is on the one hand desirable to make your own attitude clear on any matter of substance, it is on the other difficult and on the whole unprofitable to try to force the Asiatic to give a definite expression of opinion. Generally speaking, he dislikes the prospect of having to make a decision, and on the whole he tends to return the answers which he thinks his questioner expects, rather than those which correspond closely to the truth. Truth, he would argue, is after all relative."—Guidance on Foreign Usages and Ceremony, and other Matters, for a Member of His Majesty's Foreign Service on his First Appointment to a Post Abroad, *by Marcus Cheke, His Majesty's Vice-Marshal of the Diplomatic Corps (1949).*

Yes and no

It's not just in the East that people have a problem refusing others. *Nja* is a Swedish word that combines both *ja* (yes) and *nej* (no), but in fact really means no. This gentle negative has less to do with face, though, and more with the need for consensus in a famously cooperative society.

"No, no, you go first"

In Iran *taarof* is the display of extreme politeness that accompanies almost all dealings with others in everyday life. A group of men approaching a door, for example, will show *taarof* by competing to insist that the most senior of them goes through first. After a business meeting, *taarof* may mean that your counterpart insists that you don't go back to your hotel but join him at his house for dinner. In a shop *taarof* may even mean that a shopkeeper will insist you pay nothing for an item you've expressed interest in buying.

Do by all means enjoy the respect paid to you, but don't take it too seriously. "Come to my house for dinner" is the Iranian equivalent of "Let's do lunch"—only if your new associate is still insisting after several refusals might he just possibly mean it. As for shopping, there are tales told in Tehran of shopkeepers who've insisted on handing over goods to foreigners for nothing only to have them arrested for shoplifting once they've left the premises.

Not done

Nyekulturny is a Russian word that means that something is uncultured or "not done." The classic example of *nyekulturny* behavior is to wear your overcoat inside a public building—say a restaurant, theater, or concert hall. Traditionally you should leave both your coat and boots in the *garderob* (cloakroom). As concerts and the theater are still "occasions," you dress up for them.

Older people in Russia would likewise still regard it as *nyekulturny* to stand with your hands in your pockets, slouch, sprawl in a chair, raise your voice, laugh loudly, or whistle during ap-

Public displays of affection, eating lunch on a park lawn, 103 or telling someone you have to go to the toilet were all once equally frowned upon. But times are changing, and, though the idea of *nyekulturny* still exists, the new generation of Russians are unlikely to take such Soviet-style gentility too seriously.

The little way around

In Germany rules are made to be obeyed. Paying attention to street signs, waiting at traffic lights, not using a lawn mower on Sunday—there is a reason for these restrictions; they have been generally agreed on by the democratic society everyone is a part of, and one should stick to them. In other parts of the world, however, great stock is made of getting around the rules that the state or society lays down. In Brazil they have a word for it: *jeitinho*, which means "the little way around or through." *Cariocas* (those who live in Rio de Janeiro) are always looking for a *jeitinho* and will congratulate themselves when it's found. In its broader sense *jeitinho* means that there's always an alternative to the official way: humans respond to humans, palms can be greased, favors can be called in, and the tedious demands of bureaucracy and the law can be avoided.

Pragmatic

Disrespect for the law in Brazil has sometimes come from the highest echelons of society. To President Getúlio Vargas, who ran the country for most of the period between 1930 and 1954, was attributed the saying "For my friends, anything. For my enemies—the law." Another well-known politician of that time, Adhemar de Barros, was known by the cynical slogan Rouba, mas faz—"He steals, but he gets things done."

By any means

In France a not dissimilar concept to *jeitinho* goes by the name of *Le Système D*—where D stands for the French noun *débrouillardise*, defined as *l'art de se tirer d'affaire par tous les moyens* (the art of pursuing your business by any means). Getting around bureaucracy, getting ahead despite the rules, employing people at black-market rates, backhanders, favors—these are all aspects of *Le Système D*. If you are in competition with a local for anything from hard-to-get tickets to a job, it's good to bear this attitude in mind.

Baksheesh, baba!

Across North Africa and the Arab world and into Pakistan and India, *baksheesh* is a way of life. (The word comes from the Persian word for "gift.") There are essentially three kinds. The most noble is the giving of alms to the poor, an act that makes you, the giver, holier (*Baksheesh, baba!* cry the beggars in Pakistan). The second *baksheesh* is the "tipping" variety, as a thank-you for services rendered (even if you didn't want the service in the first place). That little guy at the airport who grabs your bag and helps you through customs, for example, will expect *baksheesh,* as will his mate who holds open the door and his other mate who stands in the restroom with a big friendly grin. The third kind of *baksheesh* is the one that outsiders find hardest to handle: *baksheesh* for services rendered in advance, which some would see as tantamount to a bribe.

This kind of up-front *baksheesh,* though fine for porters, attendants, drivers, and so on, should never be offered to a professional person or business associate: this will cause serious offense. In business, *baksheesh* should be given only after the give-and-take of negotiation is over, to say thank you and create a good relationship for future dealings. This is most categorically not a bribe. Bribery is dangerous and can lead to jail. Bear tip or a favor.

Petiquette

Attitudes toward animals around the world are sadly not always as soft as they are in the pet-loving United States and United Kingdom. Dogs in particular get a rough ride in the East. In Arab countries they're considered unclean, and the Prophet Muhammad (PBUH) is supposed to have said that angels will not visit any house that contains a dog. Another *hadith** proclaims that for every day you own a dog your good deeds in life are diminished. To add injury to insult, there are five animals that Islam allows to be killed in a sanctuary: rats, scorpions, kites, crows—and dogs. In Korea the species has an even worse time. Though some Koreans do keep dogs as pets, they are also reared as farmyard animals in constricting cages, before being slaughtered to make dog stew.

Though cats have historically been protected and honored across Asia, and kept as pets, there are still parts of China where they are eaten: particularly in the dish called "dragon and tiger and phoenix," which mixes cat with snake and chicken. In Korea cats are not just eaten but boiled alive with herbs to make *goyangi soju* (cat tonic), a remedy for arthritis.

Elders and betters

Old people in most societies outside Europe are highly regarded and treated with great respect. In Arab countries it's customary to usher an old person to the front of any line or to offer to stand in their place. In China you always greet old people first

---

* *Hadith* are traditions relating to the life and sayings of Muhammad (PBUH). Originally oral narrations, they were subsequently written down and are kept in a series of much-revered collections.

when entering a private house; at a table, too, the oldest person is given first choice of the dishes on offer, or the best piece of duck or chicken will be put in their bowl. Across the East everyone stands up when an old person enters or leaves a social gathering.

In India it would be regarded as rude to call someone older than yourself by their first name; you should use "Uncle" or "Aunty" instead. In the Philippines, likewise, anyone older than you should be called *Manang* or *Ate,* if female, or *Manong* or *Kuya,* if male, followed by their name (for example, *Manang Mila*). In rural Africa the elders are the most venerated people in the village, forming an advisory body to the chief.

In Japan they not only respect old people on a daily basis, but also have a national holiday to honor them and celebrate long life: *Keiro no Hi,* the third Monday of September. Only in the sophisticated West are the old marginalized and placed in residential or retirement homes on a regular basis—though Europe leads the world with its anti-ageism legislation.

Good as you

Travelers from the progressive West should remember that attitudes toward gay men and women are often nowhere near as liberal as they are at home. Homosexuality for both men and women is still illegal in a majority of countries around the world. Botswana has a seven-year maximum jail sentence, in Sri Lanka it's ten, while in Singapore, Pakistan, and Uganda, among other places, homosexuals can be put away for life. Saudi Arabia and Iran still keep the death penalty for sodomy, as do other countries and states where sharia law applies.

In startling contrast, many European countries have legalized not just homosexuality but same-sex unions. Denmark led the way with "registered partnerships" in 1989, with Norway, Sweden, and Iceland following in 1993, 1995, and 1996 respectively, Finland in 2002 and the United Kingdom in 2005. The

Netherlands became the first country to offer full civil marriage rights in 2001. Belgium followed in 2003 and Canada and Spain in 2005. In Spain gay married couples may also adopt children.

The United States is divided on the issue. Vermont was the first with civil unions in 2000, with Connecticut following in 2005. Massachusetts became the first state to issue same-sex marriage licenses in 2004, while in California a bill to legalize same-sex marriage was vetoed in 2005 by quondam gay pinup Arnold Schwarzenegger.

The *karma* of beggars

In India the unrelenting, ubiquitous poverty can be shocking to outsiders. Beggars may be hard to resist—especially small children or those without limbs or who are disabled in other ways. But bear in mind that if you do offer money, a crowd will quickly gather, and you will be swamped with aggressive demands for similar payouts. It may be hard for Westerners to accept this, but for Hindus *karma* dictates your position in society; in the next life, if you behave well, you may well have moved up from being a beggar. More controversially, your lowly status in this life may relate to bad deeds in a previous life.

In the Philippines, by contrast, everyone is regarded as deserving of the profoundest respect. Indeed, the grander you are, the more you're expected to unbend and be benevolent. If you refuse the requests of a beggar, you should do so with the phrase *Patawarin po* ("Forgive me, sir"). To ignore or push away such a person rudely would be to risk loss of face.

In Muslim countries giving to the poor and needy is one of the five pillars of the faith, particularly important during Ramadan. Walking down a street in Cairo in the late afternoon, you will see plates and rugs laid out on the pavements outside shops and businesses. At *iftar,* when dusk comes and the daily fast is broken, a free meal is available there to anyone who wants it, the more indigent the better.

Five pillars

There are five obligations that are required of every Muslim. These are known as the five pillars of Islam. They are:

1. Shahada: *professing the faith. You must testify that there is no god but God (Allah) and that Muhammad is his prophet.*
2. Salat: *praying five times a day.*
3. Zakat: *giving alms to the poor.*
4. Sawm: *fasting during daylight hours in the month of Ramadan.*
5. Hajj: *making a pilgrimage to Mecca for all those able to afford it, and participating in the special rituals that take place during the twelfth month of the Islamic calendar (Dhu al-Hijjah).*

666

Unlucky numbers are taken seriously in Japan: 4 (pronounced *shi*) sounds like the word for death, while the pronunciation of the word for 9 (*ku*) is the same as "agony," so many hotels have no room 4, 9, or 13, and a major Japanese airline, All Nippon Airways, has no seats with these numbers on its planes. The numbers to go for in Japan are 3, 7, and particularly 8. This is because of the shape of the *kanji* (character) for 8: the two strokes are wider at the bottom, suggesting better things to come in the future.

Similar superstitions prevail in China, where the Mandarin word for 4 (*si*) also sounds like the word for death. A Chinese bride wouldn't hold a wedding on a day with 4 in the date, nor should you give her (or anyone) four gifts. Lucky Chinese numbers are 8 (*ba*), because it sounds like *fa*, which means prosper-

ity and abundance, and 6, because it rhymes with the word for
"smooth."

Wind and water

In Thailand or southern China be careful what you touch or move about in a room. Many objects will have been placed according to the dictates of *feng shui* (*feng* is the Chinese word for "wind"; *shui* means "water"). Thoughtful placing of mirrors (which reflect bad spirits) and bowls of water (which attract good spirits) aims to preserve the harmony of the home or workplace.

There are other rules: the foot of a bed should never face the door of a bedroom, while the bed itself should ideally face south. The front door of a house should face east, toward the sunrise; but it shouldn't be aligned with the back door; otherwise luck (and money) will go out of the house as soon as it comes in. A house at the end of a cul-de-sac is unlucky; evil spirits can march straight up to the front door.

Feng shui has now spread to Europe and the United States, where it functions sometimes almost like a branch of interior design; bear in mind, however, that in the East the presence of spirits is taken seriously.

Singing at night

Breaking a mirror, spilling salt, and seeing black cats are bad luck in most cultures. In Russia it's also inauspicious to shake hands through a doorway, light a cigarette from a candle, whistle indoors, or go back for something you've forgotten; nor should the superstitious ever look at a mirror while sitting on the toilet.

Dropping a coin into a fountain is thought to provide you with a free wish in many cultures, but picking up coins from the same place is bad luck. In Argentina, however, finding money in the street means you'll get more soon. In Brazil they believe that you'll get rich by putting sugar in your cup before your coffee, while in Turkey if your right hand itches you'll get cash from someone you don't expect. In Japan, if you put a piece of snakeskin in your wallet, you'll become rich; but if you kill a snake, you'll lose your money.

Superstitions around finding a partner are common the world over. In Mexico and much of Latin America people believe that if someone accidentally sweeps an unmarried woman's shoe with a broom, she will never get hitched. "Three times a bridesmaid, never a bride," is a common European saying; in Taiwan being a bridesmaid just twice brings bad luck; while in Thailand they say that if you sing in the kitchen, you will have a very old spouse.

Beliefs such as this last may once have had a practical purpose. In Korea, they say that if you sing at night, snakes will appear before you (would that we could scare our neighbors with similar ideas about amplified music). In Kyrgyzstan they say that if a single woman sits in a corner she won't be married— well, it's hardly the best way for her to meet the man of her dreams.

TGI Wednesday

THE BUSINESS TRIP

What may be merely embarrassing in a social context can take on a whole new dimension if you're visiting on business. In the business class lounges of the world, many a tale is told of deals made or broken thanks to the apparently trivial requirements of the local etiquette. And though you will, of course, be given leeway as a visitor who can't be expected to understand the rules, this applies less in business, especially if you're the one trying to sell something. . . .

April fool

When scheduling meetings, remember that dates are written and understood in three different ways around the world. In the United States, the first day of April in 2008 is written 04/01/08—as it is also in Micronesia and the Philippines. In the United Kingdom, Russia, Brazil, and Argentina, however, the day comes (more logically some may feel) before the month before the year—01/04/08. In China, much of Eastern Europe, and Quebec they adhere to the "international standard" and reverse it completely, so the day is 2008/04/01.

To avoid turning up at a meeting in different months—or even years—it's probably wisest to write out the month in words: April 1, 2008, or 1 April 2008, unless of course you want to be an April fool.

TGI Wednesday

The good news is that the structure of the working week is universal; the bad is that the "holy day" is on a different day within that week. In most of the world the holy day is Sunday, most people don't work on Saturdays, and the working week is Monday to Friday. But in Israel the holy day is Saturday, many people don't work on Friday, and the working week runs from Sunday to Thursday. In Arab countries the holy day is Friday, most people don't work on Thursday, and the week runs—generally—from Saturday to Wednesday. So when an Arab says "Thank God it's Friday," he means it literally.

Seven to four

The working day is not necessarily the standard 9 to 5 of the U.S. office worker. In Scandinavian countries they start earlier, around 8 a.m., break for lunch as early as 11:15 a.m., and often finish at 4 p.m. In Poland and other eastern European countries they start after breakfast at 7 to 8 a.m., then work straight through until *obiad* between 2 and 4 p.m. In Spain and Portugal they start at 7 or 8 a.m., break for lunch at midday, then take a siesta till 4, before returning to work from 4 to 8 p.m. This pattern is repeated in Latin America and the Philippines, as well as in many other countries where the heat is uncomfortable in the early afternoon, from Greece through the Middle East and North Africa to India, China, and Taiwan. In bigger cities in many of these places, however, where commuting home for a nap is unfeasible and they have air-conditioning, many businesses have abolished the *siesta*.

Rice sleep

The word siesta *is Spanish, from the Latin* hora sexta *("the sixth hour"). In Indian Bengal and Bangladesh the afternoon nap is called* bhat-ghum *("rice sleep"), as you would traditionally eat rice at lunch while being massaged with drowse-inducing mustard oil. In China the post-lunch nap may last up to three hours and is called* xiuxi *("rest").*

Prayer breaks

Devout Muslims pray five times a day, so you may need to be flexible with your timetable to fit in their schedules. Prayer times are usually upon waking, at noon, mid-afternoon, at sunset, and before going to bed. Generally the noon and early-evening slots are the ones to be wary of in a work context. Prayers will take ten or fifteen minutes, and most businesses in the Arab world or Indonesia have special rooms set aside. If you do interrupt someone praying, there's no need to apologize; just back off quietly and wait around the corner for them to finish.

Les grands départs

Before booking your business trip, don't forget to check on the local holidays. In Arab countries nothing much is done around the two key festivals of Eid al-Fitr and Eid al-Adha (variable dates), while "Christian" countries pretty much shut down between December 23 and the start of January (the first day after New Year's generally being the "back to work" day). In Australia, New Zealand, South Africa, and South America the hot summer weather extends this break, and you're unlikely to get any serious business done until the start of February. In Europe the same applies from late July to the start of September—and the French, Italians, and Greeks decamp totally during *les grands départs* of August. In Iran offices shut down for the Nouruz New Year festival of March 21 and for several days after. The same paralysis is found in Thailand over the five days of the Songkran water festival (variable dates in April), while in Japan, Golden Week, at the start of May, is not a good time to do business; there are four national holidays in the space of seven days.

Fast work

The conventional wisdom is that the month of Ramadan is a bad time for business. People are alternately hungry and tetchy during the day, then gorged and lazy after *iftar* and the ensuing meal in the evening. But some in the Arab world regard Ramadan as an excellent time to do business—of a certain kind. Shopkeepers, for example, may be so debilitated by hunger that they lack the usual energy to bargain.

The other point to remember is that after *iftar*, life has a sociable edge. Men retreat to cafés to drink late-night cups of tea or coffee or smoke *shisha* pipes—the perfect environment to close a deal.

Dress code

For men the business uniform of dark suit, conservative tie, and dark socks is acceptable pretty much anywhere. Germans are keen on highly polished shoes, while for Italians the concept of *la bella figura* prevails: use a good tailor and dress stylishly and they will notice and be impressed. In the Middle East they will clock the quality of your briefcase and watch, while in America good dentistry impresses (the disparaging description "English teeth" says it all).

Russians, too, expect sartorial formality: gossip has it that one of the reasons Mikhail Khodorkovsky and his oil company, Yukos, were destroyed by the government was that he turned up for a meeting at the Kremlin wearing a polo-neck sweater instead of a suit and tie.

Meishi

In the United States or the United Kingdom handing over a business card to a new contact or potential associate is done in a fairly relaxed matter. You may well need to be in touch with each other—so here's your card. If you've forgotten it, it's no huge problem; an e-mail address or a contact number can be scrawled on a scrap of paper, an old receipt, or even a napkin.

But in many places, and particularly the East, the exchange of cards is a highly formalized procedure. In China, for example, your card should be taken from the breast or hip pocket of your jacket (never your pants pocket) and offered with both hands, to the most senior person first.

In Japan, when presented with a card—or *meishi*—study it for a few seconds before putting it away carefully (ideally in a smart leather card wallet). Stuffing it in a back pocket will be seen as a mark of disrespect, while dropping it is an outright insult. Your card is an extension of your person and should be in the best

TGI WEDNESDAY

condition possible. Your counterpart may well bow on the exchange, and though there's no need to bow back (see page 8), it's polite to drop your head in an acknowledging nod. Should he hiss though his teeth, don't worry: this merely indicates that he considers you important. If you're then attending a meeting together, the thing to do is line up the cards you've been given in front of you, corresponding to Suzuki-san and Koizumi-san on the opposite side. Not producing a card will be seen as a sign that you're not interested in continuing the business relationship.

Lost in translation

What's written on the card is equally crucial, especially in countries such as Italy, Germany, and Brazil, where titles are taken seriously. A translation of your qualifications into the local language on the reverse of your card is considerate and polite anywhere, and pretty much expected in China, Japan, and the Arab world. Do make sure that it's a good one, as loose renderings can confuse: the distinction between, say, a copy editor on a newspaper and the managing editor may not be obvious to your friendly local Mandarin translator. In Japan the Japanese side of the *meishi* should be organized in the traditional way: company first (the most important thing), then your rank and title, then your name, and finally your contact information. You should offer your card with your counterpart's language face up; he will hopefully return the favor with your language on top.

In a couple of places, translations can cause more problems than they're worth. In Belgium, you may become embroiled in ancient rivalries between Flemish and French speakers; likewise between Francophones and Anglophones in Quebec. But generally it's an investment worth making.

A sign of character

If you want to maximize your impact in China, it's worth thinking about adopting a Chinese name to use in addition to your Western one. It should fit your Western name phonetically and carry an attractive and upbeat meaning. When you hand over your business card with this local moniker on it, you will be far more memorable. By the same token Chinese colleagues may want you to help them choose an English name. Remember, though, the simplified forms of the Chinese characters that are now in use in the People's Republic of China are not used in Taiwan or Hong Kong.

Zong

For those from the more egalitarian societies of the United States, Denmark, Iceland, and Australia, it can be hard to comprehend how hierarchical many business cultures are. If you are used to getting into the front of a cab and calling your driver "mate," it may seem absurd, if not downright wrong, that such a straightforward approach to others of all backgrounds is not universal. But respect comes in many different forms. In China it means knowing someone's title and deferring to their rank. You do not confuse the *changzhang* (factory manager) with the *chejian zhuren* (shop foreman); nor should you fail to pay homage to the *zong jingli* (general manager). In France, Germany, and Italy, likewise, where businesses are structured vertically, respect for higher-ups is important, and your counterpart remains *monsieur, Frau Doktor,* or *Commendatore* until they tell you otherwise.

Power breakfast

Oscar Wilde's dictum "Only dull people are brilliant at breakfast" doesn't cut ice in the United States or Finland, where the early meeting over hash browns or herring and cheese on toast remains popular. But the idea of the "business" or "power" breakfast has never really caught on in France, where *le petit déjeuner* is often no more than a *café crème* and a Gauloise. The same is true of Mediterranean and Latin American countries, where they like to get over their hangovers in private. In Asia the concept of a breakfast meeting is even less popular; even to suggest such a session would border on the disrespectful.

Starter for ten

If you are invited to a business lunch, bear in mind that different cultures will approach the "business" and the "lunch" aspects of the occasion in different ways. For North Americans, Germans, and Scandinavians, focused on doing the deal and getting things done, you may be talking business even before you get to your elk *carpaccio*.

In the rest of mainland Europe, though, it's important to engage in general chitchat before getting to work: art, films, literature, sports, funny things about your home country and your counterpart's country, comparative weather in your two countries, and so on. Wait until the coffee, or, in Spain, the *sobremesa* (after-meal chitchat) to get down to brass tacks.

The personal touch

In Saudi Arabia, likewise, as in all Arab countries, business is a personal matter. You will be expected to drink tea and coffee (and more tea) with your counterpart, chatting and getting to know each other before you can even think about getting down to work. This familiarization process, during which your colleague gets a sense of what kind of character you are, may go on over several meetings.

In countries ranging from Japan and China to Turkey, Latin America, and Africa, a similar attitude toward business is the norm. You may find yourself discussing anything but the project at hand, because the character of the businessperson they are intending to work with is far more important than the product or the deal. The other side is looking to build a long-term relationship with someone they can trust—and don't mind how long it takes.

The deal or the relationship?

The deal is king
Nordic and Germanic Europe
United States and Canada
Australia and New Zealand
Hong Kong, Singapore

Let's do the deal and be friends
United Kingdom
Ireland
South Africa
Latin Europe
Central and Eastern Europe
Chile, southern Brazil, northern Mexico

We must be friends before I can work with you
The Arab world
North and central Africa
Rest of Latin America
Rest of Asia

Guanxi

One way to cut short the long, slow process of familiarization, which is so important in "relationship-based" countries, is to be introduced by an intermediary, known and trusted by, and possibly related to, your counterpart. In China such connections are called *guanxi*; this complex, untranslatable word describes not just the people and the special influence they bring but also the attached obligation. As with many other things in the East, reciprocation is the key. You shouldn't accept favors from *guanxi* unless you are in a position to return them in some way.

The power of the personal over the impersonal is recognized around the globe, much as the "old boy network" once was in the United Kingdom. In Arab countries *wasta(h)* is the word for the private influence that can help you cut through rules and bureaucracy, find jobs, get your children into college, and so on. In Israel this sort of unofficial clout is called *proteksia*, though what counts in that country is less likely to be where you grew up or who you studied with than what army unit you served in.

In Latin America you may rely on similar behind-the-scenes leverage (*palanca*) or actively go out and employ an *enchufado*— a local fixer who knows the people you are trying to work with and can act as anything from consultant to mediator.

Tatemae and *honne*

In Taiwan, South Korea, or Japan the development of important business relationships may be fast-tracked by the judicious use of alcohol. A relationship built over beer, whiskey, or *sake* may lead to a rapid improvement in trust, as the office politeness of *tatemae* (surface communication) breaks down into *honne* (what they really think). And you can afford to let your hair down; what happens in the evening is never mentioned the next day. You should never do that English thing of reprising the hilarious horrors of the night before. Even if you threw up over several salarymen at the same time—that was very definitely yesterday.

Work-life balance

Another key division in the international business world is that between those who live to work and those who work to live. The American appetite for putting work first, even to the extent of giving up weekends, will not be understood in much of mainland Europe or Latin America. Here, regular time off is regarded as essential for family and friends and a go-getting "team-building weekend" would be particularly unwelcome. In the East, of course, the Japanese take their work just as seriously as the Americans.

Corporate warrior

The first case of karoshi (death from overwork) was reported in Japan in 1969, with the death from a stroke of a twenty-nine-year-old male worker in the shipping department of the country's largest newspaper company. At that time it was called "occupational sudden death." But in the 1980s, after the publication of the book Karoshi, the media started using the word regularly to describe the otherwise inexplicable deaths of high-ranking managers who keeled over in their prime. In 1987 the Japanese Ministry of Labor began to publish statistics on karoshi and cited figures of twenty-one cases for that year and twenty-nine for the year after. But in 1990, when a liaison council of attorneys was established to look into the problem, the figure leapt: suddenly it was estimated that more than ten thousand people were dying each year of karoshi.

No *Kompromiss*

THE MEETING AND ITS AFTERMATH

Suited, booted, and with an impeccable business card translated into the right language and displaying your correct title, you have now touched down in your host country. You are all set for everything from a weird working week to the need to spend a lot of pointless downtime making friends. But that's just the start of it. . . .

In the clock-watching cultures of northern Europe and the United States (referred to by professional interculturalists as "monochronic") business sticks to a tight schedule. If invited for a meeting in Hamburg at 10:00 a.m., you would be wise to arrive no later than 9:55. In the German mindset *Pünktlichkeit* (punctuality) is a clear indication of *Zuverläßigkeit* (reliability). Similar attitudes prevail in China and Japan. But this is not a world standard. In the more laid-back societies of southern Europe, the Middle East, Russia, and South America meetings will start when they start, and not a moment before.

In these timeless, "polychronic" countries it would be seen as strange to set an ending time for a meeting. If there's much to discuss, the meeting will take longer. If you're close to finding a solution to the problem at five to eleven, why rush away somewhere else? In such cultures, in fact, if things are going well, it's positively rude to end a meeting just because you have another one scheduled elsewhere. There will be time for that *mañana* (tomorrow).

Waiting in the corridor

By the same token, even the most important bosses from time-conscious countries are unlikely to keep clients or visitors waiting for too long. Being late or, worse, making people cool their heels outside your office while you finish off other stuff would be regarded as disrespectful.

Not so in the timeless cultures of the world, particularly those that are also hierarchical. Here big bosses may well expect less important people to wait for them. This "my time is more important than your time" attitude can seriously rile people from both egalitarian and clock-watching countries. However, if you are one of these, you should endeavor to stay calm. Pointless resentment could be counterproductive, poisoning

NO KOMPROMISS

that all-important relationship. Your strategy must be: turn up on the dot and then, if necessary, use the waiting time to get on with your own work. Laptops have greatly facilitated this. Why not piggyback on your unpunctual host's Wi-Fi instead of hanging around uselessly?

A la gringa

In Mexico, if someone gives you a time and adds *a la gringa* (like the foreigner), you can expect them to be roughly on time. If they say *a la mexicana,* it's anybody's guess.

Free for all

Another big difference around the world is how focused and private your meeting will be. For those used to working in the United Kingdom, the United States, New Zealand, or Iceland, a meeting to discuss a particular bit of business will consist of a lineup of the relevant counterparts and will concentrate on the matter in hand. This is absolutely not the case in the Middle East, Latin America, or Bangladesh, where the big cheese may have an office full of all kinds of different people, family included, and take phone calls and allow other interruptions as and when it suits him.

In these countries you may also find yourself sitting down with individuals who will say nothing throughout your meeting. Do not expect or ask to be introduced to these silent people, but don't discount them, either. Smile, nod, and include. The main man may be padding out his side to look more important or, more than likely, these are his relatives or trusted friends, and he will rely on their judgment of your proposals—and more important, of you—once the meeting is over.

And now . . . our four key points

When making presentations in the Far East, be aware of auspicious colors and numbers. Avoid that unlucky green or funereal blue in PowerPoint presentations in China, and four of anything there or in Japan is just as unlucky in business as in leisure time. If you're going to make key points make them in threes, sixes, or eights. If all goes well in China and you get applause for your presentation, the correct response, as at the entrance to a banquet, is to applaud back.

Dienst ist Dienst

Be even more careful about humor in meetings than you would be normally. Though British, American, and Australian presentations often begin with a joke, it's not just the Germans who prefer to treat work with the seriousness it demands and keep the drollery for the post-work drink. *Dienst ist dienst,* they say there, *und Schnaps ist Schnaps* ("Work is work and drink is drink").

Expressive

In Japan, sitting with your eyes closed during meetings is common and is not in any way an insult. That person may well be concentrating hard to understand your English or the words of the interpreter. Or he may just have nodded off; this isn't unusual and shouldn't be taken personally.

In Asia generally, eye contact is kept to a minimum, and a full-on direct stare could be interpreted as an attempt to intimidate your counterpart or to "stare them down." Not so in the Arab world and the Mediterranean, where the reverse is the case: it's important to hold eye contact as an expression of interest; someone who doesn't meet your eye may be regarded as evasive, even untrustworthy.

These differing forms of expression tend to go hand in hand with the way people discuss things in meetings. To the reticent Japanese man Kiyoshi, the voluble Mexican or Greek may seem rude (or even angry), while Juan or Dmitri, carrying on in his usual emphatic way, gesturing elaborately, interrupting when he feels like it, may find his Japanese counterpart tongue-tied or even indecisive. Both judgments would be wrong.

Direct dealing

In general, people from cultures in which the deal is more important than the relationship that surrounds it tend to be more direct in their way of communicating. The German or Dutch businessperson can often be forthright and blunt, while the Taiwanese or Korean, always eager to avoid confrontation, will be more indirect, using silence, facial expressions, and other non-verbal ways of communicating, and never, of course, saying no.

But this correlation is not universal. The English businessperson is often deal-focused and happy to work with relative strangers but may be nonetheless infuriatingly indirect for the visiting American or Australian.

Kompromiss

Negotiating tactics vary radically around the world. The bottom line, internationally, is that you will only be sure of getting what you want if you're prepared to walk away, but the path to that crunch point is a varied one.

The Chinese, for example, are always polite but will haggle expertly and for as long as it takes to get the deal they want. Flattery, exaggerated demands, meaningless concessions, false deadlines—anything is fair game. But remember, this is a culture whose philosophical basis comes not just from Confucius but Lao-tzu, who taught that the key to life was to find the *tao*— or "way"—between two opposing forces, the middle ground.

In Russia, by contrast, willingness to compromise is seen as a sign of weakness (if not morally wrong). If you are trying to suggest such a thing, talk about meeting each other halfway or making your proposal conditional on an equivalent concession, rather than using the dreaded word *kompromiss*. And don't be put out if you find your counterparts theatrically confrontational. "Face" is not a consideration here. In order to get their way, Russians may use all kinds of strategies, from showing

---

Haramburger

It took McDonald's fourteen years of negotiations before the first Golden Arches were raised in Russia. A chance meeting between the chairman of McDonald's Canada and a Soviet Olympic delegation at the Montreal Olympic Games in 1976 culminated with the opening of McDonald's Pushkin Square on January 31, 1990. The company's patience paid off. The branch set a world record for the most successful opening day, and Pushkin Square continues to be the busiest McDonald's on the planet.

The company has never taken its global dominance for granted. The marketing of the "hamburger" has always taken account of local cultural sensibilities—the most obvious being the removal of the syllable "ham" from menus in Muslim countries. In Israel, the Tel Aviv McDonald's serves only kosher burgers, and in Mecca—yes, there is one in the holy city, run entirely by Muslims, of course—the beef is halal, slaughtered according to Islamic rite. In the Netherlands they offer veggie burgers, and in Norway salmon burgers. In go-getting Singapore the firm came up with the Kiasuburger, incorporating the Hokkien word kiasu, which is regarded as a national trait and means "afraid to be inferior."

exaggerated patience to the staging of temper tantrums and walkouts. Delaying tactics, pressure, and threats are all a normal part of the horse trading that is Russian negotiation.

Silence is golden

When talking business in Gulf countries, be prepared for the strategic use of silence. Arabs are well used to periods of communal quiet in all kinds of meetings but know how embarrassed Westerners can be made by it. If you sense that this tactic is being employed deliberately, fight fire with fire—fall silent in return.

Babel

When speaking through an interpreter, use short, clear sentences. Try to avoid idioms, which will just confuse. Pause frequently and tell the interpreter when to continue. Translating English into German, for example, takes roughly 30 percent more syllables. And focus on your counterpart, not the interpreter. He or she will be watching you closely and reacting to your expressions and body language. Don't lose sight of the advantage you can get by doing the same.

Ringi seido

Go-getting Americans complain that Germans take forever to make a decision. The Dutch, too, often go through a ponderous process, involving *poldermodel* (wide consultation) before agreeing on a definite course.

In Japan consensus is equally important. In their almost militaristically hierarchical businesses they have a system known as *ringi seido*, whereby a new *ringisho* (proposal) from any one department of the business is sent around all relevant depart-

ments as well as upward to managers, directors, and the company president. Individual comments are made on a sheet of
paper attached to the *ringisho*, and the management makes the
final decision based on those. In the complementary process of
nemawashi (going around the roots) superiors consult their subordinates informally before proceeding with new projects. As a
result of all this internal consensus seeking, decision making in
Japan can sometimes seem infuriatingly slow to Westerners.
The upside is that, once a decision has been made, employees
are generally thoroughly committed to the project and imple-
mentation is rapid.

Dotting the i's

For the deal-driven American a contract is essential and binding
and must be rigidly adhered to. For the Chinese, though, such a
document may be just the start of the long-term negotiation.
Things can change over time. Good partners must take care of
each other by being flexible. In similar relationship-focused
countries, from South Korea to Greece, a personal promise from
a trusted business associate likewise may be more fruitful than a
written contract.

Though the Russians have a similar long-term attitude toward contracts as the Chinese, they often like work in progress
to be even more recorded than the Americans, insisting on written *protokols* establishing what has been agreed to at the end of
every meeting.

E-tiquette

E-mail is the technology of globalization, so many of the informal conventions that have sprung up to dictate its best use are
universal: copying in people unnecessarily is agreed to be almost as bad as sending huge attachments without prior

consultation—especially to those who are trying to catch up with their messages on a creaky non-broadband connection in rural Tajikistan. Being bitchy about anyone on the masthead of a received e-mail is also very ill-advised: hit the "Reply All" button by mistake and watch with horror as valuable relationships are compromised forever.

The abbreviated, conversational-style greeting and sign-off of e-mail appears to be universal, too. The French, who would traditionally sign letters *Je vous prie d'agréer, Madame, l'expression de mes salutations distinguées* are now content with a mere *Cordialement*, which is even shortened to a shocking *Cdlt*. Arabs use *Aa* as a wacky version of the formal *Assalamu 'alaykum*, and the Chinese sometimes sign off with a lucky 666.

Along with abbreviation goes a bizarre increase in intimacy: Americans write "XOXO" to people they would never kiss or hug; while the English e-mail sign-off "X" is used by the most unlikely people in a work context.

Baksheesh in business

The U.S. government exacts heavy penalties, both fines and prison sentences, on businesspeople found bribing officials overseas. In the last few years, thirty-five other nations have signed up to the OECD Anti-Bribery Convention. But many other countries not only turn a blind eye to the activities of their citizens abroad, but they also allow companies to claim foreign bribes as a tax deduction.

Bribes can make things happen faster for businesses in countries where corruption is endemic. But bear in mind that the "special payments" or "commissions" sought are often not a one-time thing. Those who use the crooked route to get there quickly may pay dearly in the long run. An honest approach can, on occasion, pay dividends or even root out the corruption at source.

Honest discount

Sam Walton, legendary head of U.S. discount retailer Wal-Mart, was asked by Indonesian government officials on a visit to Jakarta why he didn't source garments or other products from Indonesia. He replied that he never bought goods in markets where bribes were required. The government reacted rapidly. The responsibility for determining the value of imports was removed from corrupt customs officials and given to SGS, a private Swiss firm with impeccable credentials. Wal-Mart then began doing business with Indonesia.

From Iceland to Chad

Transparency International, a Berlin-based group, compiles an annual Corruption Perceptions Index of countries based on a survey of international businesspeople. An interesting trend is that the countries considered to be the least corrupt are also among the richest, suggesting perhaps that poorly paid officials are more open to corruption.

Top 10 least corrupt	*Top 10 most corrupt*
1. Iceland	1. Chad
2. Finland	2. Bangladesh
3. New Zealand	3. Turkmenistan
4. Denmark	4. Myanmar (Burma)
5. Singapore	5. Haiti
6. Sweden	6. Nigeria
7. Switzerland	7. Equatorial Guinea
8. Norway	8. Côte d'Ivoire
9. Australia	9. Angola
10. Austria	10. Tajikistan

The United Kingdom was, in the most recent available survey, ranked eleventh least corrupt, tying with the Netherlands, while the United States was ranked seventeenth.

Bite the wax tadpole

Even when negotiations are over and contracts are signed, there is still plenty of room for disaster when operating in a new and unfamiliar culture. When Coca-Cola first launched in China, shopkeepers trying to come up with characters that sounded like *ko-ka ko-la* ended up with a name that meant "bite the wax tadpole." Only later did the company find another that meant "to allow the mouth to be able to rejoice." Pepsico had similar problems with their slogan "Come Alive with Pepsi," which came out in Chinese as "Pepsi brings back your ancestors from the dead." In Turkey, the launch of European hardware store Götzen was somewhat compromised by the local use of Göt, to mean "ass," while the Dublin-based makers of the after-dinner liqueur Irish Mist were perhaps foolish not to have forecast a poor launch for their product in Germany, where *mist* means "manure."

12

When with Romeo . . .

RELATING TO THE OPPOSITE SEX

In the United States and across Western Europe, contemporary customs and laws encourage people to act as if both sexes should have identical opportunities in all areas of life, only disallowing those not offered by nature. But these are in no way universal assumptions. It can come as a shock to touch down in one of those parts of the world where liberal Western attitudes are not taken for granted, and women not only dress differently from men, but are expected to behave differently, too. . . .

Better half

Westerners visiting the Middle East will probably find the attitudes the sexes have toward each other hardest to understand, as they are way out on one end of the worldwide spectrum. Arab women are generally expected to dress modestly and defer to their men, even to the point where a man may greet another man while ignoring the wife standing right beside him. Men may go out for meals and leave their wives at home, even if invited as a couple by Westerners. If a man does bring his wife, it will have been his decision. In the home the sexes are segregated, and women wait on their men.

In general, men and women who are either not married or very closely related still avoid situations in which they might be alone together, even for a short time. It's improper for such men and women to be in a room with the door closed, nor should they be in a car together—in Saudi Arabia they risk being stopped by the *mutaween* if they do (see page 45). They certainly should never go on a date together. The punishment for premarital sex prescribed by the Koran and *hadith* is a hundred lashes, and this continues to be enforced on occasion in both Iran and Saudi Arabia. Adultery attracts even sterner retribution: stoning to death.

Outsiders in the more traditional Arab countries may even get into trouble among themselves; not so long ago an American man seen kissing a female of the same nationality on the cheek inside a car was arrested by a member of the Saudi National Guard; she was deported and he was put in prison. None of which is to say that individuals don't break the rules in private. A Saudi woman writing under the name Mystique claims that the love story on her blog is fictional—but it's set realistically in contemporary Saudi Arabia, as is Rajaa Alsanea's revelatory *Girls of Riyadh*.

Machismo

Though the sexes can mix freely in Latin America, and laws against sex discrimination exist and are enforced, many men still regard themselves as top dogs—and *machismo* is something to be proud of. The upside of this is an old-world chivalry that will see doors being opened and women being ushered first into an elevator. The downside is the exhaustingly self-confident male predator. Women traveling alone in this part of the world, even on business, may consider wearing a wedding ring to discourage unwelcome attention. Even better would be a handy collection of photos of your children. A Brazilian Lothario may regard a childless married female as something of a challenge, but is unlikely to feel the same way about a *madre* ("mother"). A businesswoman who invites a male associate for a meal should ask him to bring his wife with him—or at the very least take along a female colleague.

Stepping behind

Despite its nominal historical attachment to egalitarianism, Russia, too, is a very *macho* culture. Women are seen as subordinate to men, and there are plenty who will tell you they really feel like a woman only around a "traditional Russian man." On March 8, "Women's Day," Russian men make a big effort, buying the ladies in their lives flowers, cooking them a romantic meal, and even washing up afterward. But the fact that this saturnalia exists only points to the status quo during the rest of the year. So a visiting businesswoman may still have to work hard to be taken seriously by her male counterparts; nor would hand kissing and other old-fashioned attentions lavished on her be considered condescending by those offering them. (Bear in mind that when Russians get married, the phrase for a man is *zhenitsva na devushke*, which means, "to take a girl," while for a woman it's *vykhodit zamuzh*—"to step behind your man.")

Ugandan relations

The *machismo* count is high in many parts of Africa, too. In Botswana it's only recently that women have been allowed to sit in the village *kgotla* (meeting place), where the chief dispenses justice, and in rural areas young women may still avoid your eye, having been raised to believe that it's disrespectful to look directly at a man. In parts of rural Uganda traditional wives still kneel when speaking with their husbands or other men, and even urban women bend their knees at times.

Women whipping

Among the Hamar people of southern Ethiopia male physical dominance is taken to extreme levels. When the time comes for a young man to be initiated (by jumping over a row of castrated bulls), his sisters must submit to being whipped by a group of newly initiated men known as the maz. *Nor is this the end of it. Once married, a wife can expect regular beatings from her husband if she fails in such duties as keeping the house tidy or preparing a meal.*

The rules

In the United States, where gender equality in the workplace is backed up by law and some firms even require you to consult a superior before asking a fellow employee out for a drink, you would expect dating to be run on similarly twenty-first-century lines. Not so. After a decade or three of trying out the idea of treating men as equals, going Dutch on dates, calling when they felt like it, and so on, many women have reverted to more traditional models, expecting to be invited out, paid for, and thoroughly romanced (and this despite the ridicule heaped by sophisticates on the millennial bestseller *The Rules*). There's a further twist to this old-style Stateside dating, which visiting Lotharios should take note of. A woman may offer to pay her share of the meal on a date, but if the man readily agrees, she may think less of him or even assume that he's not interested in her.

When with Romeo . . .

None of this retro courtship stuff would come as a surprise to the young (and not so young) Romeos of Italy. As any foreign female who has walked alone in Florence, Milan, or Naples can tell you, the rules in this part of the world are that the boys do the chasing. For a certain type of Italian man, flirting is like breathing. There is no shame in showing interest, and if rebuffed, he'll just try and make you laugh, buy you a present, offer to take you for a spin on the back of his Vespa—and generally persist. Only later will you discover the downside: he still lives with his mother, gets his washing and ironing done by her and, if he's really serious about you, would like to turn you into her second-best replacement.

In Spain they tend to date in groups. A young Spanish man will show his interest by immediately introducing you to all his friends. The Frenchman, by contrast, will want to get you alone in a restaurant of his choice, where he can impress you with the extraordinary *foie gras* only available there, washed down with a little something that only he and *le patron* have as yet discovered.

Dead talk

Northern Europeans tend not to put a huge value on small talk. In Sweden the phrase for such interaction is "dead talk." If and when you get involved with them romantically they may well be not just terse but candid. When you ask them how they think you look in that dress, they will tell you, in precise and not necessarily flattering detail.

Romantically mobile

In Egypt young Muslims who want to get around their restrictive social codes and taste the randomness of Western-style romance have embraced the possibilities offered by Bluetooth technology. With alluring call-signs such as BEAUTIFUL GIRL or FLIRTY BOY on their mobile phones they can avoid traditional restrictions about approaching strange women in cafés or on the street. If things go well, their only problem is working out how, later on, they can arrange for their parents to meet and sort things out properly.

Going steady

Until recently young Chinese men and women had to ask permission from superiors in their *danwai* (work units) if they wanted to get engaged or married. This rarely applies now, but if a man and woman are dating, the assumption is still that they will eventually marry. Visitors from the more casual West should be aware of this, if and when their heart is pulling them in the direction of a local.

Over the hill at thirty

In the West, likewise, dating was traditionally a stage on the road to marriage. Some cultures developed customs to emphasize this. In Germany there's still a charming event where individuals who have reached the age of thirty and have not got hitched are publicly punished. Accompanied by their friends, the offenders are taken to a local church, town hall, or opera house, where the men are made to sweep the steps while the women have to clean door handles covered with shoe polish. They can only be released from these onerous tasks when kissed by a virgin of the opposite sex, possibly one who may release them from their offensive state of singledom. An all-night party generally follows.

Wedlock

Despite the hype, the marketing, and the magazines, the truth is that marriage is no longer the norm in much of the Western world. In the United States the marriage rate dropped from 9.8 per thousand per year in 1990 to 7.4 in 2004. A similar decline has taken place in Europe. In 1970 the rate in European Union-25 countries was 7.9; in 2004 it was only 4.8. In these progressive cultures there is now no stigma in staying together without getting married, nor is bearing children out of wedlock at all frowned upon. The latest figures from the United States show 37 percent of births are now to unmarried women, of whom more than half are part of a cohabiting couple.

The mouth opener

For those who still want to go the old-fashioned route to the altar or sacred fire, the traditions are there to be taken or left. In many cultures the groom was expected to ask his future father-in-law for his daughter's hand, a formality that in the United Kingdom these days has boiled down to him possibly buying the old man a drink in the pub—and certainly not expecting the answer no.

In sub-Saharan Africa, however, not only must a man ask his father-in-law for his bride's hand, he must also compensate him for the loss of his daughter with a payment known as *lobola* (in Botswana, *bogadi*). In rural areas this payment is made in cattle and varies from four to twelve cows (sometimes a hut may be built for the father-in-law instead). Urban couples who still follow the *lobola* custom have switched to cash, and the bride-price is often the subject of lengthy negotiations between the families. To smooth the process, a bottle of brandy known as *mvulamlomo* (the mouth opener) may be placed on the table between the two parties, as a gesture; it is often not drunk.

Kitchen killings

In India, by contrast, a new bride traditionally brought a dowry with her, and this could be the cause of serious problems if it was regarded by the bridegroom's in-laws as inadequate; some even went so far as to murder new brides who didn't bring enough money with them. Dowries are now illegal, but the custom continues, as, tragically, do the "kitchen killings" (one every hundred minutes, according to Indian statistics), whereby new brides with insubstantial dowries meet with "mysterious" deaths at the hands of their new in-laws, generally involving a "kitchen accident."

This is a highly problematic subject in India. It has much to do with the sensitive complexities of families maintaining *izzat* (honor) in their community and is best not mentioned by visitors at all.

Semiarranged

At one time both Muslim and Hindu marriages were entirely arranged, and bride and groom were often strangers on their wedding day, catching first sight of each other in a handheld mirror during the ceremony. Nowadays, especially in the Asian diaspora, much arranged marriage is more like a dating service organized by the parents. People talk of "semiarranged marriage" or "arranged introduction." With the agreement of the potential groom or bride, many parents place lonely hearts ads in suitable newspapers or canvass specialized dating Web sites on their children's behalf. They will then select a suitable match, based on criteria that include caste, family background, wealth, and appearance. A meeting of the potential couple

may be arranged, with parents or—in more liberal families—
chaperones on hand. The couple may then be allowed a short unsupervised meeting or walk together. Even in the most traditional liaisons, where the bride and groom don't meet until their wedding day, they will probably have exchanged photographs and personal histories and e-mailed each other or spoken on the phone. At the other end of the scale, pretty much anything goes—there are even "love matches" involving other religions and races.

Honorable viewing-meeting

In Japan a less restricted form of arranged introduction provided a way for young people to meet each other. *Omiai* (honorable viewing-meeting) was a form of blind date where a man and woman of marriageable age were set up to meet by a *nakodo* (matchmaker). This middleman knew both parties and would not only introduce them but also stay involved if things worked out, making a speech at the wedding and advising on any marital problems that arose later.

Should you find yourself looking for love in Japan these days, you will discover that the *omiai* tradition continues but is altogether more informal. Friends or family may suggest a friend they think a particular single person might like. Photos can then be exchanged, and if both sides like what they see, a meeting will be arranged at a hotel or other public place. Parents and mediators will be present for a bit, while introductions are made and the couple find out a little more about each other. Personal histories may even be exchanged at this point. Then the couple will be left alone to talk between themselves. If all goes well, more encounters will follow, but the final choice about taking things further or abandoning ship remains firmly with the couple.

Modern *omiai* may even be arranged by companies—either those that people work for or specialized *kekkon sodanjo* (marriage consultation agencies), equivalent to Western dating agencies.

Schmuching

The Talmud states that a man may not marry a woman without seeing her first. However, among Orthodox Jews, dating between the sexes is still pretty much limited to the search for a marriage partner. A *shidduch* (match) may begin with the suggestion of a *shadchan*—someone in the community who has made matchmaking their business and who will expect to be paid if the *shidduch* is successful. Suggested partners will then be checked out by family and friends, and inquiries made about their character, prospects, and level of religious observance. If this is all considered satisfactory, the couple will meet, an occasion that should be entirely free of *schmuching* (smooching) or anything else that might lead to emotional attachment, the idea being that, if one rejects the other, there will then be no hurt feelings. If all goes well, however, engagement and marriage will soon follow. The *shidduch* has been much joked about in the Jewish community, but in these days of broken relationships its popularity is alleged to be reviving.

Golf, henna, crockery

Parties to celebrate the forthcoming marriage are common in many cultures and are usually same-sex affairs. In the United Kingdom the traditional stag party may now be a full weekend away, involving anything from a golf tournament in Ireland to the shooting of decommissioned AK-47s in Estonia. The hen night, though a custom of more recent invention, may often be wilder. Male strippers may be included, and elaborate games and risqué novelties are common.

In India things are gentler. A Hindu bride and her friends will spend an evening together painting traditional henna patterns on their hands (and sometimes feet) in an event known as the *mehndi;* sometimes a *mehndiwali* (professional henna artist) will be hired. If invited along to such a party, you should wear a long skirt in green or orange, with a shawl to cover your bare arms. Alternatively, if you have a sari and feel comfortable in it, wear that—the other girls will be dressed up in traditional clothes. Be prepared for much singing and dancing.

The Germans mix the sexes for their "letting-go" celebration, the *Polterabend* (the evening with lots of broken porcelain). If invited along to one of these, feel free to bring along an old plate or two. Friends and relatives will do the same, and the assorted tableware is smashed on the ground in front of bride and groom, with the results described in the old German proverb *Scherben bringen Glück* ("Broken crockery will bring you luck").

And the Bride Wore . . .

THE BIG DAY AND ITS CONSEQUENCES

Should you be lucky enough to find yourself at a wedding abroad—perhaps even as one of the participants—you will naturally be preparing yourself for many exotic differences, from the walking around the fire of Hindu cultures to the comical mock obstacles of France and Singapore. What may surprise you, though, are the many similarities, from hand-tying rituals to end-of-reception pranks. . . .

In Western cultures the bride traditionally wears white, a symbol of purity (the veil being the symbol of virginity). These days, when both bride and groom may have been shacked up for years with not just each other but a number of predecessors, other colors may be favored—though white, or at least cream, remains enduringly popular.

"Christian-style" white dresses are also now a big favorite in Japan, where rooms are decorated to look like European chapels and the ceremony may be officiated by a suitably European-looking "priest." (No religious orders necessary—beware lest you get roped in!) Otherwise, in the more traditional Shinto ceremony, the Japanese bride will wear a white or mixed-color wedding kimono; red and white are regarded as a happy combination. Her face will be made up white. Over an ornate hairdo will be a large white hood known as the *tsuno-kakushi* (horn-concealer) to hide the devilish "horns of jealousy" that will inevitably appear later on in the marriage. Male guests typically wear black suits, white shirts, and white ties, while female guests may wear a kimono or formal dress.

In China the bride wears red, the color of celebration and good fortune, complete with a red veil. In northern India she wears a red nuptial sari, and in many Muslim countries red *ghararas* (tunic and ruffled trousers). The only other women wearing red in these places will be the newly wedded, so as a guest you should avoid that. Wearing black or white is OK, or another bright color such as pink, orange, yellow, or green. Bear in mind that in India white is the color of peace, but also has an old association with death, as it's worn by widows and at funerals.

Lucky 11:43

In Thailand it's customary to consult an astrologer to ensure that the wedding is held at the most auspicious time on the most auspicious day. Often astrologers will give the start time to the nearest minute, which explains why Thai weddings take place at bizarre times, such as 11:43 a.m., or 3:52 p.m. As a guest there's no need to worry about this, though. Arrive early if you want to see the parade to the bride's house or the holy water ceremony. But if you don't make it till the reception, nobody will much mind—and you'll be in good company; half the other guests will be late, too.

Aspects of love

In India in 2003 astrologers decreed that planetary positions between July and October were disastrous; therefore, there were virtually no marriages during these months and the wedding entertainment industry suffered a serious downturn. By the end of November, however, the planets were deemed to be back in a highly auspicious combination. On the three days of November 27, 28, and 29, there were more than fourteen thousand weddings per day in Delhi alone. Banquet halls that had previously been empty were now full, and bands, priests, and ceremonial horses, camels, and elephants were in disastrously short supply. The whole fandango was repeated in 2006, when December 13 saw more than thirty thousand Delhi weddings in one night.

Here comes the groom

In most places the groom stands waiting for the bride, who traditionally arrives late enough to hold up the ceremony. If you should find yourself in El Salvador, however, don't be alarmed if the wedding starts without her. This is normal. As she finally enters the church, the congregation breaks into the nuptial song.

At Hindu weddings, by contrast, it's the bride who waits for the groom and his party, who arrive in a procession by foot, on horseback, or even—as in the cliché—on an elephant. Should you ever find yourself in this invidious position, you must remember to bring a garland for your bride and a coconut for her mother.

Tying the knot

Most wedding ceremonies have features to symbolize the ending of the two single lives and the start of the joint one. In Colombia, bride and groom each take a candle and with them light a new, single one. At a Jewish wedding the bridal couple drink from the same cup. In Japan, bride and groom drink *sake* from the same cup no fewer than nine times in front of the priest in a ritual called *san-san-kudo* (three-three-nine times).

In Mexico bride and groom are joined, during the service, by a rope. Cambodian tradition calls for each guest to tie a string around the couple's wrists, while in both Greek and Thai weddings the couple wear crowns that are linked together by a ribbon. In Scotland traditional Celtic weddings include the ritual of handfasting, in which the bride and groom's hands are tethered together. In Parsi weddings the priest places the right hand of the bride in the right hand of the groom and then ties them around seven times, while at conventional Hindu weddings the hands of the couple are bound with sacred thread as they pray together for lifelong happiness and strength.

AND THE BRIDE WORE . . . .

You may now . . .

At Western weddings the bride and groom traditionally kiss after they've exchanged vows. These days it's often a full-on, mouth-to-mouth smacker, frequently applauded by the congregation. At a Hindu wedding such a frank demonstration of intimacy would still be regarded as over the top. A modest peck on the cheek is fine after the *saptapadi* (seven final steps when seven vows are made), but even this would probably shock the older members of the congregation. A chaste kiss from groom to bride has also sneaked into some contemporary Muslim weddings but would undoubtedly still be considered bad form by traditionalists.

Next in line

In Mexico the bride places her bouquet in front of the statue of the Virgin Mary before she leaves the church. At Christian weddings in most other countries she takes it with her and, after the service, throws it over her shoulder toward her waiting single female friends. Whoever catches it first will be the next to be married. A variation of this tradition can be found in Turkey, where the bride's friends write their names in her shoes before her wedding. The name that has rubbed off by the end of the ceremony will be married next. In Spain there's a chance for the groom's pals; they just have to snip off a piece of his tie to be next in line at the altar. As a visitor from elsewhere, it would perhaps be foolish to be first with the scissors.

The boss

There are numerous superstitions surrounding the wedding day around the world. In Italy, if it rains, the bride will be lucky and happy (a consolation, perhaps, for a spoiled day). In Korea, if the bridegroom smiles a lot during the ceremony, he will have a daughter as a first child. At a Hindu wedding, the first to sit down after bride and groom have walked four times around the fire is supposed to be the boss in the marriage.

Not so fast . . .

Mock obstacles to the uniting of bride and groom are another quaint feature of the wedding day. In Singapore the traditional female beautician known as the *mak andam,* accompanied by members of the bride's family, will ask the groom for an "entrance fee" before he is allowed to see his newly glamorized bride. French village children block the bridal couple's route with ribbon, while in Japan a straw rope may be used "to hold her ransom."

Jumping the broom

This is not just a phrase for "tying the knot" but, in some sectors of African-American society, a wedding custom where both bride and groom jump over a broomstick, which will usually be elaborately decorated. Later it may be hung on the wall of the newlyweds' home.

Controversy surrounds both the custom itself and its origins. Jumping the broom was undoubtedly at one time a substitute wedding ceremony for slaves, who were not allowed to marry, but whether it carries connotations of slavery and should be abandoned or is (alternatively) empowering for black culture is hotly debated. Most believe the custom originated in west Africa, where the broom held spiritual significance among the Ashanti people as a sweeper away of old wrongs and evil spirits. Some, though, relate its origins to hated Scottish and Irish slave owners, as "jumping the broom" is also an old Celtic tradition.

AND THE BRIDE WORE . . . .

Mandarin ducks

Recording the event for posterity is now almost as important as the event itself. At English weddings the taking of group portraits by an over-assiduous photographer can hold up the reception for hours. In Italy they formalize this process, with a special "cocktail hour" at the start of the reception, during which the bridal party is kept apart for the photos while the rest of the guests make merry. In China newly married couples go to a park before their evening party to have their video shot: on camera, bride and bridegroom exchange a new handkerchief, which should ideally be red and feature mandarin ducks, famous for their monogamy.

Always be wary of taking photos during the actual service. This is often quietly frowned on by more devout members of the congregation, if not disallowed by the priest. But afterward, a wedding is one occasion where snapping away indiscriminately is actively welcomed around the world.

Taking care

The cutting of the cake is a universal reception ritual. As the newly married couple start walking toward the table, the guests move out of the way and hush in anticipation. The groom holds the bride's hand as they dig in the knife together and secret wishes are made. In Saudi Arabia, when the first slice is cut, the groom holds it out for the bride to taste; then the bride takes a slice and holds it for the groom to taste, as the guests applaud. These actions symbolize the fact that bride and groom have started taking care of each other.

Encomium

At some point during the wedding celebrations there are speeches. In the United States these generally take place at the "rehearsal dinner" the night before, when the relatives and friends of the bride and groom vie to say flattering and thought-ful things about why the couple are (a) so great, and (b) so great for each other. Criticism or mockery of either party is not welcome here.

Most speeches, though, take place at the reception. Australia and New Zealand follow the bizarre UK tradition where, after the bride's father has given an (often ramblingly emotional) encomium of his daughter, and the groom (and sometimes now the bride) has thanked everyone, the best man embarrasses the groom by relating disgraceful episodes from his bachelor past. In Germany, more constructively, both fathers line up to praise bride and groom, then anyone else can join in. Japanese receptions, likewise, feature numerous congratulatory speeches and toasts.

Hong bao

Most weddings involve parents and guests presenting the newly-weds with gifts. In China, family elders give them *hong bao* (red envelopes) containing money during the tea ceremony that is the climax of the wedding day. In the Philippines the bride is showered with paper money as she dances, while Mexicans and Hispanic communities in the United States have the "dollar dance," where guests "pay" to dance with both bride and groom by pinning money on them, often on a special sash. The traditional gift at a Hindu wedding, too, is money. In India, if following this course, you should make sure your cash present is an auspicious number of dollars—ending in 1.

Cash is also the right gift at a Japanese wedding. It should be in mint condition, not folded, and placed face up in a special envelope called a *shugibukuro*, which can be bought at stationery shops. You may give anything from 10,000 to 100,000 yen (*not* unlucky 40,000, 60,000, or 90,000), depending on your relationship with the bride and groom, and the quality of your envelope should reflect the amount of cash inside. You write your name on the bottom half of the front of the envelope and place it inside a purple or red square of cloth called a *fukusa.*

Don't be surprised to *receive* a little something, too. In the land of the endless gift, the bride and groom are expected to reciprocate your generosity. You will either be given a special catalog at the end of the wedding from which to choose your present, which will be sent on to you later, or else you'll be handed a goody bag or something more substantial as you leave; this is the *hikidemono*—or "return gift."

Brought to you by . . .

In the Philippines many features of the wedding—from candles, flowers, and decorations to the dress and the reception—will be sponsored by a third party. If you are asked to be a sponsor, it's a great honor, akin to being a godparent.

Hilarious pranks

The "going-away" of the newly married couple provides fertile ground for practical jokes. In the United States and United Kingdom, of course, the ushers and other spare men and women may well decorate the going-away car with shaving-cream slogans before tying empty drink cans and other amusing noisemakers to the bumpers. In Saudi Arabia the groom's male friends often go further in frustrating the departure of the happy pair, kidnapping him as he is about to leave and taking him to the desert for a picnic that may last two or three days. In France they have an old tradition of *chiverie,* where the newlyweds are subjected to post-reception pranks of various kinds: the door to the nuptial bedroom may be nailed up, honey or thistles may be put in the bed, or bells tied to the bed's springs. Alternatively, the guests may gather outside the newlyweds' bedroom and bang pots and pans, demanding to be let in for more drinks.

Wherever you are in the world it's always good to remember the universally most important person at the wedding: the bride's mother. This is her big day, and don't you forget it. If you're confused about arrangements, protocol, toasts, gifts, or the ceremonies, the best and easiest thing is to consult what Spanish speakers mischievously call the *bruja* ("witch," but used to mean "mother-in-law"). She *cannot* get it wrong.

Sometime later. Or sometimes earlier . . .

Baby shower

In Malta the tradition is that if it rains heavily on your wedding day, you'll have an easy birth with your first child. To try and ensure this result, many brides from the island deliberately choose autumn days for their nuptials, in particular St. Ursula's Day (October 21), St. Catherine's Day (November 23), and St. Lucy's Day (December 13).

Just visiting

The Akan people of Ghana do not name their babies until they have been alive for at least seven days. The just-born baby, they believe, may be only a spirit who has come to have a look at the world before returning to its own domain. So mother and child are kept inside, and there is little excitement about the birth for the first week. If the baby dies, there is no mourning. After seven days, however, the little individual has clearly come to stay. There will now be a baby-naming ceremony, or Edin Toa, involving a priest, godparents, and members of the surrounding community.

Americans, by contrast, are so confident of a good outcome that they celebrate the birth before it's happened with a "baby shower," when the friends of the mother-to-be have a party and "shower" her with gifts for her and her little one. If invited to such an occasion, you may bring anything from soothing bubble bath to baby booties. But in many other cultures, particularly in Africa and the East, such a celebration would be regarded as tempting fate; offering Mother a present for Baby before it's born is completely the wrong thing to do.

Clean cut

Jews wait eight days after birth to circumcise their male children. The newborn baby is brought into a room where relatives, a rabbi, and various key ceremonial figures are waiting. Everyone stands and says *Baruch Haba* ("Welcome," literally "Blessed is he who comes").

Now the *mohel*, or ritual circumciser, takes charge. In historical times the *mohel* was often a butcher, and circumcisions would take place in the morning, when his knives were still clean; these days he is more likely to be a doctor. In the Ashkenazi tradition, after the first group blessing, the *mohel* recites a prayer, then calls out *kvatter*, at which point the mother hands her baby to the *kvatterin* (godmother), who hands it in turn to the *kvatter* (godfather), who hands it to the *mohel*, who places it on the lap of the *sandak*, the man chosen to hold the baby as it's circumcised.

Further blessings surround the circumcision itself, after which the baby is given a drop of wine and named in a special prayer. Be careful where you sit. It's not unheard of for otherwise red-blooded males to faint when presented with a full view of this ceremony.

Haircut

You can never go wrong telling parents that their baby is beautiful, even if in reality it looks like Winston Churchill with a hangover. But suggestions that the little one could do with a trim should be made with care. In many cultures first haircuts are of key significance. Yezidis from countries including Turkey, Armenia, Syria, and Iran cut a baby boy's first locks after seven months in a ceremony called *bisk*. African-Americans have a tradition of cutting a baby's hair for the first time around their first birthday, as do Ukrainians, a custom called *postryzhennya*. Hasidic Jews wait till the child is three, when they have a ceremony called *upsherenish* (cut off). For Hindus a child's first haircut, known as the *choula*, is one of a sequence of purification rituals, and is particularly important, as the hair from birth is associated with unpleasant characteristics from past lives. The *choula* happens in a boy's first or third year, and many families will travel to important shrines to perform the ceremony.

Blinding the devil

In Greece, when you see a friend's newborn baby for the first time, you should say *Na sas zísi* ("May it live for you") or *Zoí na éhi* ("May it be strong with life"). Some people will preface this wish with a spitting sound, repeated three times. This is supposed to blind the devil and avert that same "evil eye" that worries Mexican mothers (see page 19) among many others.

Agusto

In the United Kingdom and the United States, babies are usually made to sleep alone from the start, even if in a crib in their parents' bedroom. This is not the case in many parts of the world, from Japan to Africa, where people would regard not having a small child in the marital bed as bordering on neglect. Latin

Americans have a word for the feeling that develops from this early intimacy: *agusto*—the closeness felt when snuggling up to a relative.

Seen but not heard

Attitudes toward child rearing vary wildly around the globe. In the Netherlands kids are encouraged to be independent little people from an early age, expressing their opinions and often calling their parents by their Christian names. This is not the case in the Philippines, where children are supposed to sit quietly and not interrupt adults. In this part of the world parents are expected both to apologize for and to deal with the bad behavior of their children immediately, or to take the child outside.

En famille

The French remain dedicated to the idea of children being *bien élevé* (well brought up). If her *enfant* behaves in a crass, tasteless, or ill-mannered way, *Maman* will not hesitate to point this out. Sons and daughters are expected to attend regular meals, eaten *en famille,* and may expect a telling off for an unmade bed or an untidy room. Children sent over to France on foreign exchanges should be prepared for the fact that *Papa* still rules the roost and may be considerably more authoritarian than they are used to at home.

Interfering strangers

If you visit China and take your children with you, you will very likely find them the center of general and public attention, especially if they have blond or red hair. In Russia don't be taken aback if a complete stranger comes up and tells you off for the way you're looking after your child. If it's cold, for example, and the child isn't wearing a coat or hat, you may be told in no uncertain terms that this is irresponsible. Such interference is quite usual and shouldn't be taken personally.

Bachelor Fridays

Single men who get married may, hands deep in dirty dishes or diapers, regret the loss of their carefree days out with the lads. Not so in Bolivia, where married men have regular *viernes de soltero* (bachelor Fridays), when they go out drinking and dining without their spouses. As well as talking about *fútbol* (soccer, a national obsession), the footloose *hombres* play *cacho,* a game with dice, or *sapo,* in which they try to shoot small metal pieces into the mouth of a receptacle shaped like a toad.

Cinq à sept

In France they are highly sophisticated about everything: food, wine, conversation, and, of course, sexual fidelity. If playing around in a long-term French marriage isn't exactly expected, then it is at least quietly understood. An affair is a *cinq à sept.* You don't let it ruin your life and destroy your family like those jealous Anglo-Saxons; you fit it in between leaving the office at five and returning to the wife and children for *dîner* shortly after seven.

Little wife

Thai men are not renowned for fidelity to their wives. In addition to making good use of the many appropriate facilities in their country, some wealthier Thais may set up a *mai noi,* or "little wife," in a separate home. In some circles an attractive *mai noi* is considered a status symbol, and a man may have more than one.

I will survive

Divorce is now illegal in only two countries in the world: Malta and the Philippines. After a long period of getting by with bogus marriage annulments (even the president had to resort to using this method), Chile finally made divorce legal in 2004.

The highest divorce rate in the world—5.3 couples per thousand, per year—is currently found in Aruba, a Caribbean island territory of the Netherlands, which ironically markets itself as a great wedding destination with the slogan "Bombini to Aruba!" Runner-up with 4.8 per thousand per year is the United States, where divorce is now so common that there are companies who supply customized divorce-party accessories, from a plastic ball and chain to an inflatable toy boy in a tin. The divorce party, say these experts, should aim to be a positive rite of passage. So it's an enthusiastic yes to rude cards, obscenely decorated cakes, booze in industrial quantities, the group watching of *First Wives' Club* or *War of the Roses, karaoke* performances of "I Will Survive" or "D.I.V.O.R.C.E," burning lists of all the dreadful things your ex did to you or even the marriage license, naughty games, young waiters in skimpy shorts, or banners and balloons reading *Divorced and Happy* or *Free at Last*. But a serious no to public burning of wedding photos, making abusive or obscene phone calls to the ex, doing anything that might inflict actual physical harm on the ex (or his car), videotaping the proceedings, or allowing yourself to be set up with a handsome stranger that very same night.

And the lowest divorce rate? Intriguingly it's Colombia (just ahead of Belize, Libya, and Georgia) with 0.2 per thousand per year. This is a country whose clichéd claim to fame is the cocaine trade. Is this the secret of a long-lasting marriage?

Sangomas to Samsara

ILLNESS, DEATH, AND BEYOND

Falling ill when abroad is never part of the plan, and doing the right thing may well not be uppermost in your mind as you lie prone on the sheets staring blankly out of the window at the pitiless sunshine and wondering whether it was the goat curry, the green mango salad, or that strange-tasting date paste that put you in this miserable state. Hopefully your insurance is up to date, the necessary international phone numbers are easily accessible in your wallet or passport, you have a working credit card, and there is a clinic within range. Otherwise you may find yourself discovering more about the society you're visiting than you bargained for.

But even if you never get sick yourself, it's good to understand that in many cultures illness is not necessarily viewed as a straightforward physical thing, treatable or not by the right combination of the right drugs. . . .

Sangoma

In many, particularly rural, parts of Africa, the first port of call for sick locals will be the *sangoma* or "diviner–priest," who will be consulted not only for a suggested cure, but, more important, for his understanding of who or what may have caused the disease.

*Sangoma*s find out the answers to these controversial questions by invoking the spirits of dead ancestors, whom they summon to their sacred huts by dancing, chanting, playing drums, and burning a plant called *imphepho*. Then they may well go into a trance and allow the individual ancestor to possess them, so he can speak to the patient directly. Sometimes the patients themselves are possessed, and the ancestor talks through them. On a more practical note, the *sangoma* will provide *muti,* medications of plant or animal origin, to help with everything from kidney problems to impotency. *Sangoma*s can be seen in markets across Africa, surrounded by their *muti* and often distinguished by necklaces of red, white, and black beads. They greatly outnumber Western-style doctors, and estimates suggest they are consulted first by approximately 80 percent of the indigenous population.

Shamans and *santeros*

Traditional shamans form a similar link between ancestral spirits and bad health right across Asia, from the *ghers* of Outer Mongolia to the leafy huts of Arunachal Pradesh. In Cambodia such healers are known as *kru khmer.* Similar beliefs about the origins of illness are still found in Latin America; from Cuba across Puerto Rico to Brazil, people put their trust in the power of *santeros,* priests who will take the problem of a particular illness to a specialized *orisha* (a saintlike deity).

Some cultures even accept the power of living sorcerers to induce illness or death from outside. In Laos they wear amulets to protect themselves against such people, who they believe may cast spells or even project foreign objects, such as a stone or an animal bone, into their bodies. This kind of conviction is still found among Aboriginal people in Australia and in the jungles of New Guinea, where evil men who cast spells are known as *kakua*. Traditionally they were killed and eaten, as only by digesting and excreting their brains could you be sure to have rid the world of their wicked souls.

Replicas

Traditional Mexicans ascribe illness to an imbalance of the four body humors of medieval medicine: blood, yellow bile, phlegm, and black bile. Each humor is either hot or cold, wet or dry, and cures involve restoring the correct balance. Other unusual local agues, such as *envidia* (envy), *susto* (fright), or *mal puesto* (bad luck), may require herbal treatments by *curanderos* (traditional holistic healers), who use massage, *limpias* (ritual cleansing), or prayers to sort out the problem. Another way of getting well is to place a small metal replica, a *milagro* (miracle), of the diseased body part near the statues of saints at special healing shrines; *milagros* are usually made of silver or gold and their use is widespread throughout the Spanish- and Portuguese-speaking world.

Life knowledge

For Indians, good or bad health is woven into the whole karmic picture of life—there may well be a deeper reason why you are ill. The cure prescribed will be holistic, taking into account body, mind, and soul, and based on the ancient system of Ayurvedic (life knowledge) medicine, which is still dominant on the subcontinent. Most remedies are herbal, but Ayurveda is one of the few "traditional" forms of medicine to incorporate a sophisticated system of surgery, known as *salya-chikitsa*.

Qi

Traditional Chinese Medicine, or TCM, is known in the West as an "alternative medicine." However, in China and Taiwan it's very much part of the established healthcare system. TCM is based on the time-honored philosophical concept that a healthy human body should be carefully balanced, particularly between masculine *yang* and feminine *yin* elements. The body's *qi* (vital energy) must also be flowing correctly. The pulse and the appearance of the tongue are key diagnostic tools. Cures usually involve acupuncture and herbal medicine, with some unlikely ingredients, such as ground tiger bone or deer penis. These are simmered together to make a dark soup, which, as anyone who has tried such potions will tell you, can range in taste from quite vile to absolutely disgusting. Certain foods are also supposed to have medicinal properties: shark's fin soup, for example, is thought to protect against cancer.

Good company

When illness is extreme and someone dies, the speed with which they are buried varies considerably around the world. Those from cultures originating in hot countries generally hurry to bury their dead. For Jews the funeral may take place on the very day of death and should be no more than two nights afterward. Though undertakers are used, a group known as the *Chevra Kadisha* (holy brotherhood) will take charge of the washing of the body and preparation of the corpse for burial. However long this takes, it is important that the corpse is never left on its own. Rapid burial is crucial, as the body must remain intact; Orthodox Jews believe that when the Messiah comes, the bodies of the righteous will be resurrected in the Holy Kingdom of God to be established on earth.

There is no requirement to wear black at a Jewish funeral. 162 Mourners gather outside the prayer hall at the cemetery until the *Chevra Kadisha* arrive with the body, when they follow inside. Prayers are then said, the centerpiece being the mourner's *Kaddish* (prayer of praise and thanks), usually led by the son of the deceased. After a eulogy from the rabbi, the body is taken off to the cemetery for burial. On returning to the hall it's traditional to wash your hands; there will then be more prayers.

For seven days after the funeral a period of intense mourning is observed by the bereaved. If you are invited to the home of the close family during this time, turn up when you're asked to, as there may be prayers for the deceased, after which the gathered mourners may offer condolences to the family. Bringing items of food or drink, so that they have no need to cook, is also traditional.

The Zaka

In Israel suicide bombings are attended by the Zaka, a group of specialist volunteer paramedics who rush to the scene and use highly sophisticated modern techniques, including DNA testing, to try to piece together the bodies of the murdered, so that they can receive a proper burial and remain as intact as possible for eventual resurrection on the Day of Judgment. The bomber's body is treated as well as the victims' and receives the same respect and care, for judgment remains the prerogative of God.

Without flowers

Muslims, too, bury their dead as soon as possible after death. The body is first washed in a particular way—known as *wudzu*—by family members, before being shrouded in an unsewn shirt and wrapped in two layers of white sheet. The deceased is then carried to a place where funeral prayers are said, which may well be outside on a street or in a courtyard, rather than inside a mosque. The *imam* faces the dead body and, beyond that, Mecca, while the worshipers line up behind. The body is then taken to a cemetery for burial.

Muslims are generally buried where they died, even if they are far from home. The body is laid in the grave, without a coffin if that is allowed by local authorities, facing Mecca. Family and friends do not erect tombstones, nor are they encouraged to leave flowers at the grave. Cremation is forbidden in Islam, as is overindulgence in grief. Relatives observe a three-day mourning period, while the widow mourns for four months and ten days, a period known as *iddah*. During this time she is not supposed to wear jewelery or decorative clothing, move house, or enter into any negotiation about remarriage.

Upside-down death

The rituals that follow a Japanese death show the reasons certain actions are strictly taboo during life. Everything around death is done *sakasa goto*—upside down. When the body has been washed by the bereaved family and its orifices stuffed with cotton, it is dressed in a *yukatabira* (white kimono), with the right side over the left, the opposite of how this garment is worn by the living. On its feet are placed straw sandals, a taboo gift in life. The corpse is then laid out in a special room, palms over the chest as if in prayer, head pointing north or *kitamakura:* another no-no in the living world.

A single stick of incense is burned at the bedside, and a candlestick and flowers are arranged nearby—usually the chrysanthemums that are never given in life. A bowl that the dead person used during life is then heaped with rice, and chopsticks are placed vertically in it—another strict taboo for the living.

After the wake and funeral, which take place over the next two days, the body is cremated in the presence of the family;

starting with the bones of the feet and ending with the bones of
the head, passing them in a way that should never be done with
food in normal life. Mourners bring gifts called *koden,* which are
special envelopes filled with money. The amount of money reflects the relationship between the guest and the deceased. As
an outsider, you would not be expected to bring *koden.*

Emotional

Like many African peoples, the Warumungu Aboriginals of
northeast Australia believe in expressing their grief. At their funerals they scream, gash their thighs to the muscle, and bloody
their heads with knives. For the Sikhs of India and elsewhere,
by contrast, a big show of emotion at the funeral—or *Antam
Sanskar*—is discouraged. Death is, after all, only the progression
of the soul on its journey from God, through the created universe, and back to God. Sikhs usually cremate their loved ones
and do not erect monuments.

Visiting time

The Chinese respect for their elderly extends to the deceased,
too. At the Qingming Festival, on the fourth or fifth day of
April, families visit the tombs of their ancestors to clean them
and make offerings of cooked meat, fish, fruit, and wine. They
then picnic on this food themselves, sitting near the tombs in
convivial fashion.

Stones

When visiting a Jewish grave, it's traditional to take not flowers
but a stone. Every year after the death, relatives light a *yahrzeit,*
or religious candle, and say an anniversary *Kaddish* for the deceased, which is repeated also on Yom Kippur.

Turning in their graves

In Madagascar the local religion takes ancestor worship a step further. The Merina and Betsileo people have a practice called famadihana (turning over the dead), where the remains of dead relatives are removed from the family tomb and rewrapped in new silk shrouds before "taking part" in festive ceremonies in their honor, involving singing, dancing, and parading of the bodies, at the end of which they are returned to their graves.

Resurrected wives

Devout Christians believe that the souls of the dead go on to eternal life—the righteous join God in heaven, while sinners are sent to hell. Some believe this happens immediately after death, with a "particular judgment" of the Almighty, others that dead souls will sleep till the Day of Judgment, when the fate of all will be decided.

The afterlife is central to Islam, too. Life on earth is seen as part of a greater journey, as well as a test; on the last day all the souls that have ever lived will be brought before Allah for judgment. Those who have led a good life will be admitted to Paradise, characterized as a garden, where they will sit on "gold-encrusted thrones of happiness, facing one another in love." Immortal youths will wait on them with goblets, and they will drink water from "unsullied springs," and eat "the flesh of any fowl they may desire." Whether they will also enjoy the company of the seventy-two virgins so beloved of the Western media is debatable. In one highly regarded translation of the Koran the companions of the good are their spouses, "resurrected as virgins, full of love." (Some commentators dispute the interpretation further, believing that the key word *hur* should be translated from the Syriac—not the Arabic—where it means "white raisin," rather than "virgin.")

166

Heaven on earth

Though Judaism puts more emphasis on life on earth than Christianity or Islam, some Jews also believe that the human soul is immortal and will survive the body, going on to *Olam Haba* (the world to come). On earth, meanwhile, others await the arrival of the Messiah. When He comes, the righteous will return to Israel, which will live free among the nations of the earth. God will overthrow the Holy Land's oppressors, the Temple in Jerusalem will be rebuilt, war and famine will end, and there will be an earthly era of peace and prosperity, culminating in the bodily resurrection of the dead in a Kingdom of Heaven on earth.

Come again

Hindus believe in one God, Brahman the Supreme, but they have no otherworldly Paradise to look forward to. They believe instead in reincarnation—*samsara*—whereby individual souls return to earth in new bodies, either human or animal, the level of their return dependent on actions taken in life. This means that life on earth is in itself an afterlife of a previous life, so those of low caste or status may be considered to be as they are because of bad actions in a previous life. After many lives the individual soul may grow disillusioned with the limited happiness offered by worldly pleasures and seek a higher, spiritual peace or *ananda*. At this point they will cease to be reborn and achieve *moksha,* or salvation, which is the individual soul's ultimate goal.

Letting go

Buddhists, too, look for happiness in a future life rather than a future place. In the absence of an almighty creator, they believe that the purpose of life on earth is to develop compassion for all living beings without discrimination and to work for their good, happiness, and peace. The aim of the individual is to accept the Four Noble Truths, which hold that life means suffering; that suffering comes from attachment to worldly things; that it's possible to end suffering by avoiding attachment; and that the way to do this is to follow the Eightfold Path of Right View, Intention, Speech, Action, Livelihood, Effort, Mindfulness, and Concentration. With all that in place, one day, possibly many lives on, the individual soul may achieve enlightenment.

Pure land

In Japan the indigenous religion of Shinto was traditionally based on the worship of nature and the souls of dead ancestors. *Kami* (local spirits) were guardians of awe-inspiring natural features: mountains, rivers, waterfalls, trees, distinctive rocks, and so on. Apart from subservience to the emperor, Shinto has few doctrines, restrictions, or taboos, focusing instead on a distinction between the pure and the impure. These are not contrasting concepts, like good and evil, or truth and falsehood, for the impure can become pure.

After 538 CE, when Mahayana Buddhism arrived in Japan, elements of the old religion combined easily with the new. For Japanese Buddhists the world that humans live in is one of six states of being (the second highest). In your next life, you may come back as a hungry spirit in *gaki,* the second-lowest realm; an animal (third lowest); a human; or a god (highest level). The judgment takes forty-nine days. By the time of the *Shijuku Nichi Hoyu* memorial service, which takes place at the end of this period, your fate has been decided. If you have sunk a level or two, and become, say, a monkey, doing the right thing is now surely more important than ever.

Good-bye, Meat

FESTIVALS AND HOLIDAYS

Whatever we believe, there's little doubt that the underlying—or lingering—faith of a country reaches its most social expression in its festivals, with their often bizarre mixtures of religion, tradition, and superstition.

Seeing a society in party mode is also a wonderful way of understanding it better. It's not until you've watched a bunch of teenagers running through the backstreets of Jerusalem in Purim fancy dress, or been drenched by blue plastic buckets of water at the Thai Songkran festival, that you really start to feel you're more than just a visitor. . . .

New Year's Day, the Festival of St. Basil: January 1

The theme of good luck and future prosperity links the numerous ceremonies and festivals of New Year's Day. Italians give oranges to friends, families, and neighbors, while in Brazil, if you eat lentils on January 1, you will make good money for the rest of the year. In Switzerland men dress up with leaves and nuts as forest spirits (or *Klauses*) and yodel their way around the villages. In Greece the Festival of St. Basil is more important to children than Christmas. They leave their shoes by the fireplace in the hope that they will receive the gifts that children in other countries got a week earlier.

For the Japanese, the New Year—*Shogatsu*—is the most important event of the year, and most people return to their hometowns and spend a few days with their families. On New Year's Day they traditionally receive *nengajo* (New Year's cards), not only from friends and relatives but also from bosses, business partners, favorite restaurants, and so on, for *nengajo* are seen as very important in building and maintaining relationships. In rural communities, people pray in front of bags of rice for a good harvest or white paper cutouts of fish and nets for good fishing.

As a guest from elsewhere, you may join in with the *nengajo,* but do please beware of *mochi,* the traditional pounded rice cake, which can stick in the back of your throat and choke you. This is no joke: several people die each year in Japan choking on *mochi.*

Say *Akemashite omedeto gozaimasu!* (Japanese)—"Congratulations, the New Year has come!"

Twelfth Night, Epiphany, Three Kings' Day: January 5–6 (Christian)

One of the three major Christian festivals, along with Christmas and Easter, Epiphany commemorates the manifestation of Jesus Christ to the Gentiles and traditionally marked the begin-

ning of the carnival season preceding Lent. The evening preceding it is Twelfth Night, the occasion of the very last Christmas
parties, after which decorations are supposed to be taken down.
In Latin American countries January 6 is the *Día de los Reyes*
(Three Kings' Day)—more important for children than Christmas itself, as this is the time when gifts are exchanged. The next
day, January 7, is the Feast of the Nativity, celebrated as Christmas in the Eastern Orthodox Church.

Shrove Tuesday, Pancake Day, Mardi Gras, Carnival: *February 5** (Christian)

Falling the day before Ash Wednesday, in the United Kingdom
this is known as Pancake Tuesday because fats, which were traditionally prohibited during Lent, had to be used up—so pancakes are cooked. In some rural areas "pancake races" are still
held. In French, the day is known as *Mardi Gras* (Fat Tuesday);
Mardi Gras celebrations are held in several American cities, no-
tably New Orleans. In the rest of the world this is the end of the
carnival season, celebrated most famously in Rio de Janeiro.
(*Carne vale* means "Good-bye meat.")

The next day, Ash Wednesday, is a day of public penance in
Roman Catholic countries. Palms blessed on the previous year's
Palm Sunday are burned. The priest takes the resulting ashes
and marks a cross with his thumb on the forehead of each wor-
shiper.

Tet Nguyen Dan: *February 7* (Vietnamese)

The most popular festival in Vietnam, celebrated since at least
500 BCE, Tet marks the start of the lunar New Year and the arrival of spring. The aim of Tet is to begin the year in the right

GOOD-BYE, MEAT

* Italics indicate that the date of this holiday varies from year to year. All dates
in this chapter apply to 2008.

way. On the eve of the three-day festival, houses and ancestral graves are cleaned and a ceremonial meal is prepared. A special dish of rice and meat in banana leaves (*banh chung*) is left on home altars so that dead ancestors can enjoy the holiday, too. The altar holds two red candles, one for the sun and one for the moon, while incense represents the stars.

Tet is a time to pay off debts, resolve conflicts in relationships, and generally move on. New clothes are worn. Firecrackers are set off, and there are races, contests, and dancing, including the traditional dragon dance. Many Vietnamese believe that washing your hair or showering during Tet will wash away good luck for the following year. Nor should parents scold children, or children cry. Older people give money to unmarried children in red envelopes.

Say *Chuc Mung Nam Moi!*—"Good wishes to you for the New Year!"

Chinese New Year, Spring Festival:
February 7 (Chinese)

Known in the West as the Chinese New Year, in China itself this fortnight is called the Spring Festival. It begins at the second new moon after the winter solstice and ends on the fifteenth day with the full moon.

Each of the fifteen days has a significance and a tradition. On the first, people abstain from eating meat, which is supposed to ensure long life. On the second, married daughters visit their parents while others are kind to dogs—this is supposed to be the birthday of all dogs. On the fifth, known as *Po Wu,* people stay at home to welcome the god of wealth. The seventh day is *Renri* (everyone's birthday), as the Chinese do not celebrate individual birthdays. The thirteenth day is a cleansing day, when only rice congee and *cai xin* (greens) are eaten. On the fourteenth day preparations are made for the Lantern Festival, which is held on the fifteenth night. On the stroke of midnight every door in the house must be left open to let out the old year. Older relatives and married couples give red envelopes (*hong bao*) containing money to younger unmarrieds; the money must be an even number, to distinguish from the odd number given at funerals. Should you feel inspired to join in, eight dollars is particularly lucky.

Say *Gong Xi Fa Cai!*—"Congratulations. May your wealth increase!"

St. Valentine's Day: February 14

Not a national holiday but celebrated around the world, this special day began with an ancient Roman fertility festival and was recast in the late fifth century CE as a Christian feast day in honor of St. Valentine (though there are at least three different early saints of that name). Only later did it become associated with romance, and it is now thoroughly secularized—a day for lovers to send cards to secret fancies and for men already in relationships to demonstrate their continuing adoration of their partners by buying them red roses or taking them out for costly candlelit dinners. Even in Japan they observe this day of compulsory romance, though here it is the women who are encouraged to give heart-shaped chocolates, not just to their boyfriends or husbands, but to all the other men in their lives, bosses included. These are called *giri-choko* (duty chocolates), and are distinct from those *honmei-choko* (true feeling chocolates) given to lovers and friends. Husbands, intriguingly, are often in receipt of *giri-choko*.

Say *Ai shiteru* (Japanese)—"I Love You."

St. Patrick's Day: March 17 (Irish)

The big Irish national day honors St. Patrick, patron saint of Ireland, and is an excuse for Guinness-swilling parties in Irish-themed pubs the world over. In America they drink "green beer," a brew dyed the Irish national color, while major cities host annual St. Patrick's Day parades, attended by a splendiferous array of appropriately dressed American Irishmen, some of who have never set foot on the gloriously verdant sod of the Emerald Isle.

Say *Sláinte* (*duine a ol*)—"Cheers (to one and all)."

Purim (Feast of Lots): *March 21* (Jewish)

A day of feasting, Purim celebrates the deliverance of the Jews in the fifth century BCE from a massacre planned by the Persian prime minister Haman. According to the Book of Esther, the beautiful Jewish queen Esther interceded with her husband, King Ahasuerus (Xerxes I), to spare the life of her cousin Mordecai and all the other Jews of the city of Shushan. Haman was then hanged on the same gallows he had built for Mordecai. The holiday is marked by the reading of the Book of Esther (the megillah), the exchange of gifts, dressing up in fancy dress, and giving donations to the poor. On Purim it is said to be incumbent on a Jewish man that he get so drunk that he cannot distinguish between the names Haman and Mordecai.

Say *Chag purim sameach*—"Happy Purim." Later try "Haman and Mordecai."

Nouruz: March 21 (Iranian)

The Iranian New Year, Nouruz (New day, new life) takes place at the vernal equinox and lasts for thirteen days. Fires are lit and may be jumped over by the more excited revelers. Yogurt, garlic, eggs, and wheat are placed on plates in front of mirrors in guest rooms and the *haft seen* (seven S's) table must be set with seven traditional items beginning with S: *samanoo* (sweet wheat pudding), *sumac* (dried crushed berries), *serkeh* (vinegar), *seeb* (apple), *scar* (garlic), *sombol* (flowers), and *senjed* (the dried fruit of the oleaster tree). Besides these, the special Nouruz table should also contain a bowl of goldfish, a Koran, pomegranates, pictures of relatives, brightly colored hard-boiled eggs, and ninety-four coins in a dish, which are taken away by the guests for good luck.

Say *Eide shoma mubarak!*—"Happy celebration!"

Easter: *March 21–23* (Christian)

On Good Friday, which starts this sequence of holy days, hot cross buns are traditionally eaten as Christian churches commemorate the Crucifixion with long services and vigils. Two days later Easter Sunday celebrates the Resurrection with joyful hymns and the giving of chocolate Easter eggs. In Poland, where Easter is a weeklong festival, eggs are painted with beautiful patterns and placed in the center of the Easter table, alongside a small sugar lamb holding a cross and sometimes a roasted pig's head. The eggs are cut into slices and exchanged with wishes of good luck and prosperity for the coming year. On Monday the season ends with *Smigus Dyngus,* a delightful custom where Polish men wake up the unmarried girls of the district by spraying them with water.

Say *Wesotego Alleluja!* (Polish)—"Alleluia for Easter!"

Magha Puja: *March 21** (Buddhist)

A public holiday in Thailand, Magha Puja commemorates the day when the Lord Buddha ordained 1,250 *arahantas* (monks) and gave a sermon known as "Ovadha Patimokha," which laid down the main precepts of his teaching. Colorful ceremonies take place throughout the country and the much-revered king attends the royal Temple of the Emerald Buddha. In the early morning food is prepared and offered to monks; later incense and flowers are taken to temples; in the evening there are candlelight processions.

* Dates vary among countries.

Vaisakhi: April 14 (Sikh)

The Sikh New Year festival is based on a long-established harvest festival in the Punjab. The day also commemorates 1699, the year when the tenth guru, Guru Gobind Singh, chose to transform the Sikhs into a family of soldier saints, known as the Khalsa Panth—the Pure Ones. The festival is marked with *nagar kirtan* (town singing) processions through the streets, during which *shabads* (divine hymns) from the Guru Grath Sahib, the Sikh holy book, are sung.

Songkran, Chaul Chnam Thmey, Pi Mai: April 13–15 (Buddhist)

This festival marks New Year in Southeast Asia. Water is splashed over Buddhist statues, monks, and other people, as a blessing and for fun. As with the earlier Chinese New Year, houses (and home altars) are decorated with flowers, balloons, and streamers. Children give money or presents to their parents. Local communities feed local monks, and then feast among themselves afterward.

Say *Sur sdey chnam thmey!* (Cambodian)—"Welcome the New Year!" *Sawadee Pi Mai!* (Thai)—"Happy New Year!" *Bun Pi Mai!* (Laotian)—"Happy New Year!"

Passover (Pesach): April 20–27 (Jewish)

The Feast of Passover commemorates the escape of the Jews from Egypt. As they fled, they ate unleavened bread, and from that time Jews have allowed no leavening in their houses during Passover. Houses are swept of all crumbs and normal bread is replaced by crispy *matzo*. This is a time of new beginnings, when traditionally houses are spring-cleaned from top to bottom. In Israel schools are closed during the weeklong festival and businesses work half-days.

Golden Week: April 29–May 5 (Japanese)

This string of national holidays kicks off with Showa Day, the birthday of former Emperor Showa (Hirohito). Constitution Day follows on May 3, when the new, postwar constitution is commemorated. May 4 is Greenery Day and May 5 is Children's Day, when people hoist *koinobori* (cloth carp) on poles outside their houses, while inside they place *gogatsu ningyo* (warrior dolls) in helmets and armor to which they offer *kashiwamochi* (oak-leaf-wrapped rice cakes) and *chimaki* (boiled rice cakes). Visitors should make sure they have booked ahead, as this is a very popular time for vacations in Japan. With four holidays in a single week, it's also obviously not a great time for business.

Vesak: *May 19* (Buddhist)

Buddha's birthday is celebrated across the Far East on the first full moon day in May (or June, in leap years) and is also known as Visakah, Waisak, Buddha Purnima, Phat Dan, Saga Dawa, Vixakha Bouxa, and Ka-sone. On Vesak, Buddhists commemorate the birth, enlightenment, and passing away of Gautama Buddha. They meditate, reaffirm their faith and "radiate loving-kindness." In Sri Lanka all liquor stores and slaughterhouses are closed for two days. Elsewhere, flowers, candles, incense sticks, and vegetarian food may be brought to shrines. This is a good day to head to your nearest temple with a few coins and join in with the spiritual vibe.

Bon, Obon: *July 13* (Buddhist)

Buddhists visit family tombs on this day and pay homage to the spirits of their ancestors, particularly those who have died the previous year. Incense is burned to symbolize the burning away of one's self-created delusions. Floating lanterns are sent down-river or out into the ocean, representing guides for souls as they journey back to the spirit world. In Japan more lanterns illuminate public dancing areas, where women dance barefoot in *geta* (wooden clogs) and *yukata* (blue and white costumes) to the rhythmic beat of the *taiko* (drums). The Japanese give each other gifts called *ochugen* during this time. These are household necessities such as cooking oil, hand towels, instant coffee, seaweed, or canned soup, but always boxed and beautifully wrapped. Traditionally, such presents were for parents, teachers, bosses, and other superiors, but nowadays a wider range of people receive them. As a visitor, it's a nice and respectful gesture to give *ochugen* to your hosts.

Ramadan: *September 2* (Muslim)

Commemorating the first revelation of the Koran, Ramadan is the start of the monthlong fast that all Muslims are supposed to keep during the daylight hours. They must abstain not only from all food and drink, including water, but also from sex and smoking. They should also try to avoid evil thoughts, demands, and actions, some of which can annul the fast (lying, slander, a false oath, or a glance of passion all do so).

When visiting Muslim countries during this period, remember that it's regarded as bad manners to eat, drink, or smoke in front of someone who is fasting; if you must eat out in the day, do so at an international hotel. You can always stuff your face at the meal that follows *iftar,* the moment at dusk when the fast is broken with a drink of water or milk and a date.

Rosh Hashanah (Jewish New Year): *October 1* (Jewish)

This is the start of the Ten Days of Penitence, when Jews examine their relationship with God (while God decides who will live and die during the coming year). In synagogues on this day, a ram's horn called the *shofar* is blown after three special groups of prayer. The horn relates back to Abraham's near-sacrifice of his son Isaac (as opposed to Isaac's brother, Ishmael, in the Muslim tradition). On the evening before Rosh Hashanah, *challah* bread and apples are dipped in honey to symbolize the hoped-for sweetness of the coming year.

Say *Shana Tova!*—"Good New Year!"

Eid al-Fitr: *October 2* (Muslim)

At the sighting of the new moon, the ninth month of Ramadan is over and it's time for Eid al-Fitr (Small Eid), one of the two key feasts of the Muslim year—as important to Muslims as Christmas is to Christians, with a similar emphasis on family get-togethers and feasting. People dress up, and children are given gifts of money or clothing. A special compulsory contribution called *zakatul* is also paid at this time—a specific amount of food or money to provide a meal for someone in need. Party clothes are worn, and special prayers are said. On this day, as with the other larger Eid, it's customary to congratulate a Muslim and send a card if you know them well.

Say *Eid mubarak!*—"Happy Eid!"

Yom Kippur (Day of Atonement): *October 9* (Jewish)

This holiest of Jewish days marks the end of the Ten Days of Penitence that began with Rosh Hashanah. It is described in Leviticus as a "Sabbath of Rest" and is a day of total fasting—from sundown to sundown. In Israel nobody drives, and television and radio stations shut down. On this day it's traditional for Jewish men to wear the *kittel*, the white robe in which they will one day be buried.

Say *Gmar Hatima Tova*—"May you be well written in the Book of Life."

Diwali (Divali, Dewali, Deepavali): *October 28* (Hindu)

Diwali is the five-day festival marking the Hindu New Year, also known as the Festival of Lights, as important to Hindus as Eid or Christmas is to other traditions. Homes are cleaned, windows are thrown open, candles and lamps are lit, and doorsteps are decorated with colorful powders to welcome Lakshmi, the goddess of wealth. Old business accounts are settled and new books are opened. Diwali cards are exchanged and a vegetarian feast is shared by the family. Diwali is particularly important to Sikhs as it also celebrates the release from prison of the sixth guru, Hargobind Singh, in 1619.

Say *Sal mubarak!* (Gujarati)—"Happy New Year!"

Halloween: October 31 (Christian)

The eve of All Saints' Day, Halloween is traditionally associated with customs such as bonfires, masquerading, and the telling of ghost stories. In Ireland, Halloween is the big fireworks night, and in some places people put on fancy dress. The city of Derry hosts a particularly spectacular party, with people dressed up as everything from the pope to terrorist gunmen. Be careful not to tuck in too heartily to the traditional colcannon, a dish made from cabbage, potatoes, and milk, which is served with a ring, a coin, a thimble, and a button inserted into it. Whoever finds the ring is supposed to be married within the year; the coin symbolizes future wealth; the button, bachelorhood; and the thimble, spinsterhood.

All Souls' Day, Día de los Muertos: November 2 (Christian)

Following hard on the heels of All Saints' is the day when Catholics remember their dead. In Mexico this "Day of the Dead" is the country's biggest festival, and many believe that ancestors return to earth. On the days preceding, families clean and repair graves and decorate them with *coronas,* wreaths of real, plastic, or often paper flowers. Photographs of dead relatives are placed on specially constructed *ofrendas* (home altars), along with flowers and special food and drink in black ceramic bowls. This includes *pan de muerto* (bread of the dead), which may be shaped like corpses or decorated with crossbones made from dough, as well as favorite foods of the deceased relatives. Meanwhile *calaveras de azúcar,* skulls made from sugar, often wrapped in brightly colored tissue paper, are given as gifts.

Thanksgiving: *November 27* (American)

The big nondenominational day of thanks across the United States and among the American diaspora is marked by the consumption of turkey and of pumpkin and pecan pies. It's always observed on the fourth Thursday in November.

Eid al-Adha (Feast of the Sacrifice): *December 9* (Muslim)

The most important feast of the Muslim calendar, Eid al-Adha concludes the annual *hajj,* or pilgrimage to Mecca. It lasts for three days and commemorates the willingness of Ibrahim (Abraham) to obey Allah by sacrificing his son. According to the Koran, Ibrahim was about to put his son on the altar when a voice from heaven stopped him and told him to sacrifice a ram instead. Muslims believe the son to be not Isaac, as told in the Talmud and Old Testament, but Ishmael, who is considered to be the forefather of the Arabs. Eid is a day of thanks and appreciation of life, and in particular a day for forgiveness, when people attempt to resolve long-running personal conflicts and reach necessary compromises.

Say *Eid Mubarak!*—"Happy Eid!"

Hanukkah (Festival of Lights): December 22–30 (Jewish)

This festival dates back to 164 BCE, when the priest Judas Maccabaeus rededicated the defiled Temple of Jerusalem, desecrated three years earlier by Antiochus Epiphanes, who set up a pagan altar and offered sacrifices to Zeus Olympius. According to the Talmud, only a one-day supply of nondesecrated oil was found in the Temple when Maccabaeus prepared it for rededication by removing all Syrian idols. Incredibly, the oil lasted for eight days; the miracle is commemorated by the lighting of the Hanukkah candles, which are placed on the *menorah,* a nine-branched candelabrum. During Hanukkah, people give children coins or small change, while the kids themselves traditionally play games with the *dreidel,* a four-sided spinning top.

Christmas (Feast of the Nativity): December 25 (Christian)

The most widely celebrated holiday of the Christian year, Christmas is observed as the anniversary of the birth of Jesus. Traditional Christmas customs range from the Victorian innovations of plum pudding and the Christmas tree (first set up in Germany in the seventeenth century), to the exchange of gifts and the hanging of mistletoe, originally a Druid ritual marking the winter solstice (in pagan tradition, last year's mistletoe is burned and replaced with a fresh bunch, which symbolizes hoped-for peace and good fortune in the coming year).

Say "Merry Christmas."

New Year's Eve: December 31

The end of the old calendar year and the start of the new is celebrated in most cultures. It's a time for forgetting the disappointments and failures of the previous year and looking forward to better things in the next. In parts of rural Ireland a loaf or cake is taken outside the house and hammered against closed doors and windows to drive out misfortune and let happiness in. In Denmark front doors are banged on to "smash in" good luck for the New Year. In Spain, with each gong of the clock at midnight, the Spanish put a grape into their mouths; the twelve grapes eaten symbolize good luck for each month of the New Year.

The first over the threshold after midnight is also supposed to bring luck. Many cultures welcome a tall, dark stranger, though in Scotland, where "first footing" is a well-observed tradition, doctors, ministers of the church, and gravediggers are not acceptable, nor are those whose eyebrows meet in the middle. In the Deep South of the United States, which has an identical custom, good fortune can also be brought by good-looking women, children with birthdays on New Year's Day, new brides, or mothers. So if you're in a party with any of these, make sure to push them to the front.

Say: *Feliz Año Nuevo!* (Spanish), *Prosit Neujahr!* (German), *S Novim Godom!* (Russian)—"Happy New Year!"

Kill the *Saudades*

WHEN YOU STAY TOO LONG

Eventually there comes the moment when your visit abroad can no longer be described as a visit. You may not have fallen in love, got married, or died, but you have nonetheless become part of the place. It no longer feels odd to hear people saying "G'day!" "Y'all," or *Konichiwa,* or to see them slurping their soup or spitting on trains. That initial sense of novelty, in which you delighted in every difference of your new abode while simultaneously being thrilled that underneath, these oddly behaved people were essentially the same as you—essentially human—has worn off. You start to become frustrated, depressed, or worse—how very, very different these weirdos are with their grubby habits, disgusting food, and infuriating ability never to be on time or say no when they mean it. You are in the throes of what the pioneering Finnish anthropologist Kalervo Oberg called "cultural shock" and has since become known as "culture shock." . . .

And then . . .

As novelty fades and you enter this typical second stage of irritability and hostility, it's important to remember that "home sweet home" does not necessarily offer the only right way of doing things. Don't obsess or grumble about what you miss; focus instead on what you've gained. Perhaps, after all, cheese or salami are nice things to eat for breakfast. So what if they've never heard of hash browns or pancakes with maple syrup? And is a cold Bud really so great? Warm English beer and hot Japanese sake have their moments.

Gradually you will move on to the third stage of being in a new culture: adjustment. You will start to notice subtle aspects that explain previously worrying things. In Russia, for example, where the language has no definite article, you may have found people rather on the abrupt side with their blunt demands. Now you will start to realize that their language has other ways of being polite. Finally you will move to what professional interculturalists recognize as the fourth stage of being abroad: adaptation and biculturalism, when you are able to operate well in both cultures. You will start to treasure ways of saying and doing things that you're definitely going to miss if and when you ever leave.

Gezelligheid

The Dutch word *gezellig* translates as "cozy" or "congenial," but *gezelligheid* goes far deeper than that, describing not just the enjoyment of the company of others but also a deeper sense of living harmoniously with them. Community spirit is a key part of Dutch life, the only downside being that of a village: nosiness and a feeling that it's OK to criticize neighbors, whether because they have an untidy garden or their children play the drums too loud on a Friday night.

The *craic*

The Irish have a similar desire to have fun with other people, summarized in the concept of the *craic*. In an age when there are Irish bars offering *craic* in Azerbaijan, Chile, Hong Kong, and Thailand, to name but a few, the concept borders on the clichéd. But *craic* is still real enough in Ireland: a word that defines exulting in the moment, surrounded by others, having a wildly enjoyable time. But this isn't all, for the *craic* has a gossipy element to it, too, as in "What's the *craic*?" or "Didja hear the *craic* about Mary?" One anonymous bar philosopher once defined *craic* by describing it as an acronym of the following five Gaelic words: *ceol* (music); *rince* (dance); *amhrain* (songs); *inis scealta* (storytelling), and *cainte* (gossip).

Certainly it represents the pure essence of a certain type of Irishness, and, like the black stuff, is never quite so good away from the Emerald Isle. So if you're over there, and hear that the *craic* at a party is going to be "mighty," go.

Sabai sabai

Thais like to enjoy life, too. People, the feeling goes, should make time to kick back and chat, eat, or just sit around. Even the harder things in life, such as work, should aim to be *sanuk* or "fun." *Sabai sabai*, which literally means "well well," takes on a deeper sense of "calm," "easygoing," "comfortable," "happy," and "cool" to epitomize this chilled-out, hedonistic attitude, which as a *farang* (foreigner) you should take full advantage of.

Yoyuu

Yoyuu is a word that perhaps captures what is unique about Japanese culture at its best. What does it mean? Mental and emotional space, flexibility, leeway, room to breathe. As you al- low yourself to be in this state, perhaps joining your new Japanese friends for a picnic under a blossoming cherry tree in springtime, you can repeat to yourself *Ichi go ichi e,* an expression that means that each and every moment you live is special, the only one of its kind, in your and everyone else's life. Treasure it. Life is transient; experience is fleeting; to be spontaneous is the best way of making the most of things.

Saudade

Saudade is a Portuguese word for a feeling that is not expressed in any other language. The simplest translation is "a longing for something that was or might have been," and it's the "might have been" that distinguishes it from mere nostalgia. *Saudade* carries the hope that what has gone may one day return, even as the hoper realizes that this is unlikely or impossible. You might feel *saudade* for a lost love, a distant place where you were once happy, a loved one who has died, even feelings and moods that you had in your youth but have grown out of. To listen to a singer in a Lisbon bar belting out the *fado* with her eyes flutteringly half-closed is to get near to the feeling of *saudade*—and the heart of the Portuguese, both the homegrown lot and their New World cousins the Brazilians. Which is not to say that they are all forever mooning about in a wistful state; in Portugal there's a strong desire to *matar as saudades* (kill the *saudades*), and a popular Brazilian song, the first *bossa nova,* is "Chega de Saudade" ("No More *Saudade*").

Hüzün

Hüzün is a Turkish word that can be simply translated as "melancholy" but which means far more than that. Turkish Muslims experience *hüzün* when they have, as Orhan Pamuk puts it in his book *Istanbul,* "invested too much in worldly pleasures and material gain." If only they had remained on a more spiritual path, they wouldn't care about such loss. For the Sufis of that country, *hüzün* is an even more positive sadness: the spiritual anguish a person feels because they cannot be close enough to Allah, or do enough for him in this world.

Ubuntu

In southern Africa, from Mozambique through Zimbabwe and on into Botswana, South Africa, and Namibia, there's a deep sense that life is meaningful only if lived for and through other people. This is summed up by *ubuntu,* a word that has no direct translation into English: "I am because we are" or "A person becomes human through other people" perhaps get closest. This longstanding tradition of humanity toward others lies behind the extraordinary acts of forgiveness that were witnessed by South Africa's Truth and Reconciliation Commission.

Forgiveness

The South African Truth and Reconciliation Commission was set up by the Government of National Unity in 1995 to investigate the gross human rights abuses that had taken place under apartheid. Though much criticized in some quarters, the proceedings of the three main committees led to some extraordinary scenes: victims confronting their torturers, and murderers admitting their guilt and being granted amnesty (though the substantial majority were refused). Between April 1996 and June 1998 the hearings were publicly presented on South African television every Sunday.

Utang na loob

Utang na loob, which translates loosely as "the debt of obligation," is central to Filipino society (at least among the Tagalog-
speaking lowlanders) and describes a complex system of
reciprocal obligation. This applies not just to the giving of gifts
but also to assisting people in many varied ways. You might put
in a good word for somebody at work to help them get a job or
assist them financially when they're ill or moving house. This
then creates a state of indebtedness, and consequent obligation,
in the helped family, which can continue over generations.

Lagom

In pragmatic Sweden the concept of *lagom* is central. It means that
nothing should be done to excess or taken to extremes; the best
course is always the sensible, middle one. People shouldn't try to
stand out. Everyone and everything should be *lagom*—that is,
"just right," "reasonable," "in balance." People should work and
be paid "just enough" to live comfortably but modestly. The
Swedish social welfare system follows *lagom:* those who earn much
more than normal are taxed progressively higher to pay for those
who earn much less. *Lagom är bäst,* they say—"*Lagom* is best."

Janteloven

In neighboring Denmark (despite the old rivalry between the
two countries) a similar spirit of egalitarianism prevails. The
Danes talk about *Janteloven* (the law of the Jants), originally
thought up by the Danish-Norwegian author Aksel Sandemose,
who, in his novel *A Fugitive Crosses His Tracks,* listed ten laws designed to keep people in their place in the imaginary Nordic village of Jante. *Janteloven* means that ostentation is frowned on,
and anyone flaunting their success or thinking they are better
than others should be cut down to size.

Sisu

The adjacent Finns, however, put great stock on the concept of *sisu*, which is variously and loosely translated as "courage," "guts," "pride," "pluck," and so on, and refers to the quality of standing up obstinately or determinedly to keep your independence and get what you want, particularly in adversity. Competitors in the Sauna World Championships obviously need *sisu*, as do those competing in the annual Wife-Carrying or Air-Guitar Championships. And Finland itself, of course, displayed enormous *sisu* in standing up to the might of the Russian bear over many a long year.

Thumbs-up

At Finland's Sauna World Championships participants are pitted against each other in enduring a sauna of ever-rising temperatures starting at 230°F. Half a liter of water is poured on the stove every thirty seconds. To prove they are still alive, competitors have to give a thumbs-up sign to the judges at regular intervals; the last one to run from the sauna wins. In 2002 the men's winner, Leo Pusa, demonstrated exceptional sisu, *lasting in the intense heat for twelve minutes.*

IBM

Despite the differences between the separate areas of the Arab world, from the Fertile Crescent of the north, through the oil-rich states of the Gulf to the North African Maghreb, it's still generally true that it doesn't do to rush things. There's a widespread, fatalistic attitude that whatever will happen will happen, for the best, as God wills. This is summed up by the acronym IBM: *inshallah* (God willing—something will only happen if Allah wills it); *bukra* (tomorrow—things take as long as they take); *ma'alesh* (don't worry—however things look now, they will turn out for the best).

In a street-corner conversation in most Arab cities you could get by almost indefinitely with a good shoulder shrug and these three words.

She'll be right

Although—or perhaps because—they live in a country where they are surrounded by natural hazards and creatures that are seriously life-threatening, Australians have a similarly laid-back attitude, summed up by the cheery phrase "She'll be right." Initially you may think that they're just being upbeat and optimistic, but as you see them plunging into a sea full of sharks, sea snakes, killer box jellyfish (laughingly nicknamed "stingers"), and deadly stonefish, crying, "She'll be right!" you start to realize there's a good deal of fatalism about their approach as well. As a visitor, there is absolutely no shame in not following their advice.

Ni modo

Across the Spanish-speaking world, and particularly in Mexico, the phrase *ni modo* represents an extension of these attitudes of leaving things to fate. Oh well, whatever, no big deal, it couldn't be helped, there really isn't a choice, there's a bigger power out there, we humble humans can't control everything. *Ni modo* releases us from unduly blaming ourselves or one another. It acknowledges that nature will take its course, timing is everything, and that what is meant to be, will be. If you try and cross Mexico by public transport, you will have plenty of moments when the *ni modo* state of mind is a lifesaver.

Do Svidaniya, Darling

SAYING GOOD-BYE

Saying good-bye is often difficult, but never more so, perhaps, than with the people you've met while abroad,
whether locals or fellow travelers. Often an e-mail address
or telephone number is exchanged, as a token of the
warmth of your encounter as much as anything else. Secretly, or not so secretly, you both know it's unlikely to be
used. And that if it is, meeting up for a hurried drink one
cold night at home is never going to be the same as the
lazy laughs you've shared drinking caipirinhas in the cool
shade of the beachside bar. . . .

Go well

Most cultures have a variety of good-byes, from the short-term *Hasta luego* ("See you later") or *Hasta pronto* ("See you soon") to the more permanent *Adios*, which, like good-bye, itself derives from a phrase meaning "God be with you."

Many languages offer a hope that the journey onward will be safe. In South Africa this is the meaning of the gently musical *Sala sentle* of Tswana, *Sawubona* of Nguni, and *Sala gashi* of Sotho, echoed by the somewhat blander "Go well" of English-speakers in that country. Farther north, in the Chinyanja language of Zambia and Congo, *Endani bwino* means much the same, as does *Safari njema* in the Kiswahili of Kenya.

Hello, good-bye

In the Hebrew of Israel, *Shalom* means three things: "Hello," "Good-bye," and "Peace." The Hawaiians have a different emphasis: *Aloha* means "Hello," "Good-bye," and "love." In Italy, *Ciao* can mean "Hi" or "Bye," and in Finland *Hei*, too, is fine for both greeting and departing.

A final misunderstanding

Gestures for good-bye are not universal. In Greece, to avoid confusion with the offensive *moutza* (see page 17), you wave good-bye by extending your arm, palm upward, and then moving your fingers back and forward—the exact same gesture as the American or English "come here." Confusingly, this gesture is widespread in Italy, too.

In other parts of Europe and Latin America the classic good-bye wave of the United Kingdom and the United States—flat palm outward, side to side—doesn't mean good-bye, it means no. In these places the good-bye gesture consists of an arm outstretched, palm down, hand waving up and down from the wrist.

DO SVIDANIYA, DARLING

Group wave

In countries as different as France and Saudi Arabia it's important, when saying good-bye to a group, to do so to every individual present, ideally with a handshake. The cheery American "group wave" is not a world standard.

And so we say . . .

Arabic	*Ma'salama*
Bengali (Bangladesh)	*Shuva-bidhai*
Dutch	*Tot ziens*
Estonian	*Head-aega*
Finnish	*Hei, näkemiin*
French	*Au revoir*
German	*Auf Wiedersehen, tschüß*
Greek	*Adio, Geia*
Italian	*Ciao, arrividerci*
Japanese	*Sayonara, bye-bye*
Latvian	*Sveiki, a'taa*
Malay	*Selamat tinggal*
Mandarin Chinese	*Zai jian*
Norwegian	*Farvel*
Polish	*Do zobaczenia*
Russian	*Do svidaniya, Poka*
Swahili	*Kwaheri, safari njema*
Thai	*Lar-korn*
Turkish	*Hoscakal*
Yumpla Tok (Torres Straits)	*Siyu*
Zulu	*Ngeyavalilisa, Sala kahle*

Kikokushijo

Your worst problem now will be when you descend through the scurrying gray clouds, touch down, slide to a halt on the gleaming runway, trudge down miles of soulless corridors, hear the horribly familiar accents of home—and experience reverse culture shock. Your sentimental memories of the good ol' country are rudely replaced by the reality. You have grown used to a place where people grin as they greet each other on the street, where good-looking members of the opposite sex catch and hold your eye, where children with nothing squeal with happy laughter as they play with toys made from coat hangers, where people care for their elderly and an invitation to dinner in a restaurant means a *free* dinner. Without even realizing it, you have become what the Japanese call *kikokushijo*—someone who has lived abroad and has difficulty fitting in when they return.

But that's a different story. . . .

Further Reading

Intercultural studies began seriously in the 1960s with the work of Geert Hofstede and Edward T. and Mildred Reed Hall, whose books *Culture's Consequences* (Sage Publications, 1980) and *Understanding Cultural Differences* (Intercultural Press, 1990) are seminal, defining such key concepts as "monochronic" and "polychronic" cultures (Hall and Hall), "uncertainty avoidance" (Hofstede), and so on. Anyone serious about coming to grips with this subject should read these writers before moving on to such anthropologists and interculturalists as Fons Trompenaars, Robert T. Moran, William B. Gudykunst, Andre Laurent, Simcha Ronen, and Oded Shenkar. Other intercultural experts have joined the fray more recently, generally adding their own attempts at systematizing the complex cultural differences of the world. Two books in this category are *Mind Your Manners* (Nicholas Brealey Publishing, 2003) by John Mole, inventor of the Mole Map; and *When Cultures Collide* (Nicholas Brealey International, 2005) by Richard D. Lewis, inventor of the Lewis Model of Cultural Types.

On a more practical note are the guides intended for the traveling businessman. In the United States, Roger E. Axtell's *Do's and Taboos Around the World* (Wiley, 1985) is helpful, as is *Kiss, Bow, or Shake Hands: How to Do Business in Sixty Countries* (Adams, 1994) by Terri Morrison, Wayne A. Conaway, and George A. Borden, and the comprehensive Global Etiquette series by Dean Foster (Wiley, 2000). Gwyneth Olofsson's *When in Rome or Rio or Riyadh* (Intercultural Press, 2004) is perhaps the most accessible to a general reader, particularly because the material isn't broken down country by country. *A Survival Kit for Overseas Living* (Nicholas Brealey Publishing, 2001), by Robert Kohls, is also full of good insights.

Kuperard Publishing's Culture Shock! series of "customs and etiquette" guides to individual countries are useful for the single-destination traveler and have been followed more recently by their Culture Smart! quick guides, which are likewise interesting on a country-by-country basis. For the Middle East, I also found Margaret Nydell's *Understanding Arabs* (Intercultural Press,

2006) helpful, as well as *Don't They Know It's Friday* (Motivate Publishing, 1999), by Jeremy Williams. Hedrick Smith's *The New Russians* (Random House, 1990) is a fascinating follow-up to his first book, *The Russians* (Times Books, 1983). On contemporary China I can recommend Xinran's *What the Chinese Don't Eat* (Vintage, 2006) and on Japan, Simon May's *Atomic Sushi* (Alma, 2007).

Selected Sources

p. 9 "Les bises": *What the Chinese Don't Eat* by Xinran (Vintage, 2006), pp. 11–13.

p. 12 "Gestures": *Gestures: Their Origins and Distribution* by Desmond Morris, Peter Collett, Peter Marsh, and Marie O'Shaughnessy (Stein and Day, 1979); *Gestures: The Do's and Taboos of Body Language Around the World* by Roger E. Axtell (Wiley, 1991).

p. 17 "Le Camembert": Ile-de-France Regional Committee of Tourism, Paris, http://www.cestsoparis.com.

p. 21 "Piropo": these examples and their translations come from a much longer list at http://www.cyber-tango.com.

p. 35 "Bangalored": *Observer*, April 25, 2004; *Sunday Times*, October 17, 2004; *Christian Science Monitor*, November 23, 2004; *Guardian*, November 6, 2006; see also *The Queen's Hinglish: How to Speak Pukka*, by Baljinder K. Mahal (Collins, 2006).

p. 36 "Bonjewer Monsewer": for American/Chinese mix-ups, see Axtell's *Do's and Taboos Around the World* (Wiley, 1985), page 16.

p. 45 "Going Native": for Togo beads, see Axtell's *Do's and Taboos Around the World*, page 4.

p. 47 "Czechiket": *Prague Post*, November 16, 2005.

p. 48 "What can you buy for $19.99?": United States Office of Government Ethics, Subpart B, "Gifts from Outside Sources," *Standards of Ethical Conduct for Employees of the Executive Branch*, Sec. 2635.204.

p. 56 "The right glasses": these examples of German toasts appear, with others, on About.com: German language (http://www.german.about.com).

p. 64 "Ch'a": *Tea 4 You: A Brief History of the Nation's Favourite Beverage*, UK Tea Council.

p. 69 "Offering joy": this "meal verse" by Thich Nhat Hanh appears with others in *Dharma Rain: Sources of Buddhist Environmentalism*, edited by Stephanie Kaza and Kenneth Kraft, (Shambhala, 2000), p. 449.

pp. 70, 76 "Stalin's spoons" and "Sheep's eyes": quotes from "Diplomatic Dinners," BBC Radio 4, 2006; reported in BBC News, October 10, 2006.

p. 88 "Corrective": National Library Board, Singapore; http://www.ExpatSingapore.com.

p. 92 "Road accidents": *The Economist Pocket World in Figures 2007* (Profile Books, 2006).

p. 103 "Pragmatic": BBC News, December 14, 2005; *Financial Times,* May 22, 2007; *ReVista: Harvard Review of Latin America,* Spring 2006.

p. 106 "Good as You": International Lesbian and Gay Association, World Legal Survey; also Homosexual Rights Around the World (http://www.actwin.com/eatonohio/gay/world.htm).

p. 121 "Corporate warrior": *Karoshi* edited by M. Hosokawa, S. Tajiri, and T. Uehata: (Roudou Keizai Sha, 1981); *Karoshi—Death from Overwork: Occupational Health Consequences of the Japanese Production Management (Sixth Draft for International Journal of Health Services)* by Katsuo Nishiyama and Jeffrey V. Johnson, February 4, 1997.

p. 131 "From Iceland to Chad": Transparency International is at http://www.transparency.org.

p. 134 "Better half": see www.inkaleidoscope.wordpress.com/tag/mystique-saudi-arabia and *Girls of Riyadh* by Rajaa Alsanea (Penguin, 2007).

p. 136 "Women whipping": see *Tribe* by Bruce Parry (Michael Joseph Ltd., 2007), chapter 8, passim.

p. 138 "Romantically mobile": *Daily Telegraph,* January 14, 2007.

p. 139 "Wedlock": 2005 figures from Federal Interagency Forum on Child and Family Statistics, published July 2007 at http://www.childstats.gov.

p. 146 "Aspects of love": BBC News, August 1, 2003 and November 27, 2003; *Guardian,* December 14, 2006.

p. 166 "Resurrected wives": Quotes from *The Message of the Qur'an,* translated and explained by Muhammad Asad (Book Foundation, 2004), Sura 56:15–22, 34–7. For commentary on *hur,* see "Virgins? What Virgins?" by Ibn Warraq, *Guardian Review,* January 12, 2002, and *Die Syro-Aramäische Lesart des Koran: ein Beitrag zur Entschlüsselung der Koransprache* by Christoph Luxenberg (Das Arabische Buch, 2000).

p. 184 "Cultural shock": see "Cultural Shock: Adjustment to New Cultural Environments," in *Practical Anthropology 7,* pp. 177–82, 1960, and *Survival Kit for Overseas Living* by L. Robert Kohls (Nicholas Brealey Publishing, 2001), pp. 91–9.

p. 187 "Hüzün": see *Istanbul: Memories and the City* by Orhan Pamuk, translated by Maureen Freely (Knopf, 2005), pp. 81–96.

Acknowledgments

In compiling this book I have consulted—among others—the books mentioned in Further Reading and am grateful to all their authors for those observations and insights I've added to my own. Likewise, my thanks to all those who've answered my endless questions in intercultural and other chat forums on the Internet. Also, of course, to those numerous kind people who've tolerated my traveling faux pas over the years, from Zululand to Santiago. For inspiration, suggestions, checking of facts, insider's knowledge, and much more, I am indebted to many others, in particular Amir Amirani, Stephen Barber, Vanora Bennett, Benedict Flynn, Naomi Gryn, Dave Ho, Daniela Krautsack, Georgina Laycock, Alice Mogwe, Parish Parmar, Kimiko Pulsford, G.T., Mike Tsang, and Jan van Maanan.

Thanks, as always, to agent Mark Lucas for deal making and wise counsel; to my British editor, Daniel Crewe, for encouragement and meticulous work on the manuscript; and to copy editors Matthew Taylor and Trevor Horwood, and all the rest of the switched-on team at Profile. In America, I'm grateful to agent George Lucas, and all the guys at Holt, David Patterson, Patrick Clark, Rita Quintas, Michelle Daniel, Dana Trombley, and the rest of the team, who've eased this text so gracefully across the pond. Finally, for love, support, and a few good backpacker's insights, too, my wife, Jo.

Index

About the Author

MARK McCRUM has visited six of the seven continents (not Antarctica), and written several books. He has been mugged in Rio, picnicked on a glacier in Chilean Patagonia, and lunched with the king of the Zulus, a strict teetotaler whose manners were impeccable. McCrum lives in London.